Preaching as Theatre

Preaching as Theatre

Alec Gilmore

SCM PRESS LTD

0 334 02650 4

First published 1996 by
SCM Press Ltd
9–17 St Albans Place London N1 0NX

Typeset at The Spartan Press Ltd
Lymington, Hampshire
Printed in Great Britain by Biddles Ltd,
Guildford and King's Lynn

Contents

If you want to hear the music
    listen for the bass line
If you want to see the picture
    look at the spaces
If you want to understand the conversation
    listen to the silences
                (Anon.)

Preface

If I were asked to say what more than anything else drove me into the ministry, I think I would have to say that it was the desire to preach. Like many others, I 'cut my teeth' in the pulpits of Burnley, Rochdale and the Rossendale Valley before I left school, and in spite of all the varied demands of the ministry over forty years, that aspect of the work has had an unfailing attraction for me, not only as the most appealing but also as the most important. Fortunately, what I preach today bears little relation, either in style or in content, to what I preached then, and this is not entirely due to a changed world or to the fact that over the years I have changed and see things differently. It is more because about half-way through my ministry I landed on something which I knew I had been neglecting.

Up to that point I suppose I would have argued that I was exercising a teaching ministry in the pulpit. Thanks to my early training in Manchester University, under Manson and Rowley, I knew the importance of good biblical scholarship and of including something in every sermon that the majority of the congregation might otherwise not have known about. Thanks to the influence of Kenneth Dykes at the Manchester Baptist College (as it then was), I knew the importance of preaching that was prophetic in the best sense – relevant to the world we were living in, opening it up and not being afraid to raise questions and subject what was going on to positive criticism in the light of scripture.

But this preaching was always essentially cerebral. Not necessarily learnèd. Sometimes incredibly simple, and at worst trite. Had I not always been taught to preach so that the simplest person in the congregation could follow? Had I not been brought up to laugh at the preachers of whom it was said, 'I couldn't understand a word he said but I'm sure he's very clever'? But it was still brain to brain. The preaching was subconsciously intended to start in mine and finish in theirs. Nobody had passed on the quip from Descartes that 'feeling is thinking', and I never quite grasped the point that my listeners were people before they were brains. A whole dimension was missing.

A number of things brought about the change. One was the importance of planning not just the sermon but the whole act of worship in such a way as to create interest and stimulate thought. That taught me that people who had difficulty with sermons often found it easier to latch on in a different place, at a different level and with a different part of their being, which in turn then led them to appreciate the force of the sermon in ways they might otherwise have missed. I explored that in my Edwin Stephen Griffith Memorial Lectures at Cardiff Baptist College 1973,[1] and with students at the Louisville Baptist Seminary, Kentucky, where I served as Visiting Professor in the summer of 1974.

A second factor may be described as the discovery of drama. My reading in the late 1960s, such a good period in British theatre, told me that the great biblical and theological issues were being increasingly handled on the West End stage and had always been present in the best dramatists. Several books[2] opened up these concepts, and ever since I have found myself turning increasingly to Arthur Miller, Tennessee Williams and Edward Albee, as well as re-discovering T. S. Eliot, Henrik Ibsen, Samuel Beckett, Anton Chekhov and their like, to see how their interpretation of the prophetic voice contributed to that of scripture and vice versa. How did each provide balance to the other?

Thirdly, I had the benefit of two patient, tolerant and stimulating congregations who not only gave me the freedom to experiment but contributed to the process. At Kingsthorpe, Northampton (1952–62), I had the benefit of people who always had their feet on the ground and for whom the test of a good sermon was not only whether it was a fair expression of the faith but also whether it said something to their situation. At West Worthing (1962–74) I had the benefit of a people more given to intellectual activity, plus a tension between those who wanted to stick to 'the faith once for all delivered to the saints' and those who were looking for new forms of expression and inspiration. The acid test for the former was whether what was said in the pulpit had a firm biblical foundation. The acid test for the latter was whether it 'rang bells' for them. The tension proved creative in a number of ways, but it was when we developed the church theatre group[3] that I discovered two foci I had been missing.

One was that when a group of people see a play each sees it differently. Not only does one see details which another misses, but sometimes their descriptions of the play afterwards leave you wondering if they have all been to the same event. It is not simply that they come out with different interpretations as to its meaning. It is more that at each point, because of who they are and where they have come from, their sympathies and antagonisms fall in different places. The play therefore is neither what it was when it left the author's desk nor even what it was when the director and cast put it on the stage; it is what the life and experience of its audience make it. I coveted more of this for preaching.

Through this experience I came to see that there was no definitive meaning to a play and perhaps therefore no definitive meaning to scripture or a sermon either. Discovering what it meant originally, or in its first manifestation, was never really possible and probably not very significant even if it were. It took its meaning from its setting and its hearers. Arguing in the theatre group about what a play meant might be interesting and informative. We could learn from another by listening to one another. But in the last resort what it really meant was what it meant for me.

The other focus, arising from this, was the realization that the best drama was not so much about changing my mind or my opinions or making me think about things, as about touching my feelings and changing the way I lived. For members of the theatre group the impact of the play was always less in what it *taught* them and more in it what it *did* to them. Of course they would talk about it. Of course they learned something from it and from one another as they discussed it. Of course the play continued to live for them in the theatre group discussions, though they had done all kinds of other things in the two weeks that passed since they saw it. However, what mattered was not the ideas but their response, their feelings, attitudes and reactions as a result of experiencing it. In some cases all this happened before they left the theatre, and though they were very happy to share other people's impressions and insights as well as to contribute their own, the 'event' was not something to be debated, discussed, accepted or rejected, certainly not to be modified. Something had happened. One might almost say 'God had spoken'. How, then, could we achieve this by preaching?

Evangelical preachers had always said something like this about preaching – more warmth, less head, more heart – but then they had always so narrowly related it to a fairly small and very limited set of spiritual experiences. The theatre was different. The theatre touched life in its fullness.

Fourthly, whilst all this was going on, I was regularly in and out of the BBC and ITV studios working with a variety of producers on different kinds of programmes. I was with Peter Brooks, writing and presenting 'Seeing and Believing', which was Sunday morning worship that was more like drama than your traditional Sunday morning service, and 'Meeting Place', which was the fruit of a worship workshop. I was with Roy Trevivian and Crispian Hollis, producers of Prayer for the Day, and David Winter and Frank Topping, producers of Pause for Thought, from all of whom I learned much about presentation. But probably what influenced me most in this world was not so much what any individual said or did as the constant exposure to a whole world which thought and operated so differently from the church.

Two decades after *Tomorrow's Pulpit* therefore, and with the advantage of further exploration and experimentation, the purpose of this book is to present preaching more as an art form than as an academic lecture, 'political' statement, doctrinal teaching or homily. It is a search for more theatre, less classroom; more *perception* of facts with which one is already familiar than new knowledge or information; more to increase awareness, less to present ideas; more to touch a chord, less to stimulate a brain or exhort a will. And the end-product is not a carefully constructed theory based on systematic research, but rather an account of a journey and the sites explored on the way, thus leaving readers to determine for themselves how much is of value to them.

Preaching as Theatre is not a 'how-to-do-it' book, as though one had suddenly stumbled on a new method which worked when all the others hadn't. Nor is it intended to be critical of other methods and approaches, though for the purposes of clarification it may at times appear like that. It is much more concerned to highlight something which has always been around but has not received too much attention, in the hope that readers in general and preachers in particular may find it helpful, and that some at least will be stimulated to take the ideas further.

The method and style have presented some problems. What I did not want was a book of theory with occasional illustrations which by their brevity were open to misinterpretation. But neither did I want a book of sermons with the briefest of theoretical introductions and no attempt to focus on structure. I have therefore tried to strike a balance between *theory*, for those who have to teach or who wish to examine in more detail the finer points of the architecture, backed up by reference to other sources and adequate illustrative material; *raw material* for those who are hunting for ideas; and *hints and suggestions*, for those who want to develop the idea for themselves.

The overall theory and its setting in the world of pulpit, biblical and theological scholarship is in the Introduction and Chapter 5, whilst the Appendix handles one or two of the basic ideas which are especially important for this way of doing things. Chapters 1 to 3 then contain sufficient theoretical material for each chapter, together with illustrative material, roughly in a proportion of one to three; and Chapter 4 provides ingredients and recipes (or at least suggestions) rather than finished products, for those who have been captivated by the idea, want to go further and would welcome a start.

The large amount of raw material is deliberate. It is to demonstrate the variety of ways in which the overall concept may be explored as well as to provide sufficient detail for readers to mull it over for themselves and run the risk of it suddenly taking them off in a quite different direction. Indeed, only if the concept does that may it be said to have succeeded! It is intended to spark off other ideas and open other doors. In other words, this is not a book to abandon because you find in it something with which you disagree or something not quite right; better to launch out in your own boat and see where it takes you.

This left me with the difficult decision, however, as to how much raw material should be quoted in full. In some cases it proved necessary to quote at considerable length because the meaning and message depend so much on the careful choice of language. Some drama refuses to be summarized, and if you wish to demonstrate the finer points of the text, you cannot do it by just telling the story plus the punch-line. In other cases ideas can be summarized very well, and the summary is more helpful to those who wish to explore further than the full text could ever be. What matters there is the end. Sometimes it is not necessary for the reader to distinguish between the idea being explored and the text of the sermon. I have therefore tried to ring the changes for variety and to choose a method most appropriate to the sermon in question.

A further difficulty relates to the background. BBC repeats, especially where comedy and satire are concerned, often depend on an explanatory note reminding the viewer of the circumstances at the time. This can be irritating, but it can also add to the enjoyment and is sometimes absolutely necessary to understanding. If this were simply a book of sermons, there would be no case for sermons which were obviously dated. But it is not. It is a book on preaching theory with an abundance of illustrations, and since a fundamental part of its philosophy is that preaching must be related to local time and circumstance, it is inevitable that some of the illustrations require that kind of background note. I have therefore retained some sermons in that category because they demonstrate what I am talking about.

As to the style, I have tried as far as possible to be objective, so as to allow the ideas and principles to come through. However, this was not possible throughout, because some of the actual material is personalized either in itself or in its setting or selection. At such points, therefore, the first person singular takes over. I can only hope that this factor will be appreciated and will not detract from the overall presentation.

Whilst on a personal note, if this book were to receive a dedication, then it would have to be to those two congregations to which I have referred and to a limited number of churches who have found what I had to offer to their liking and where I have preached regularly. Most of all, though, it would have to be dedicated to Enid, my wife, and Ian and David, my sons, who have been my greatest inspiration, have fed me freely with ideas, books, plays, films, etc. which otherwise I would surely have missed, and who remain my sharpest critics.

Finally, the reader. I see the audience as students and teachers of preaching, ministers, clergy and lay people of all denominations, and that limited number of lay people who have an interest in preaching and 'enjoy' a good sermon.

Introduction:

Making Something Happen

Depending on the listener, 'the theatre' may conjure up opera, drama or music hall, whilst Theatreland may be Leicester Square or the West End, the local Rep. or even the street. Similarly with preaching. To a tub-thumping Baptist evangelical it may mean fifty minutes with the congregation hovering over hell, to a liberal Anglican not more than thirteen minutes of gentlemanly discourse, and to a Roman Catholic possibly a brief five-minute homily. It is therefore important first to set our scene.

The principal of a theological college, shortly before retirement and obviously feeling the pressure of teaching his students how to preach, asked his wife, who had spent a lifetime listening to sermons, what she regarded as the mark of a good sermon. She thought for a moment and then said, 'The test of a good sermon for me is whether it makes me want to be a better person.' Her answer is interesting as much for what it doesn't say as for what it does. She was largely indifferent as to what he chose as his text or his topic, whether he worked to a lectionary or a pattern of his own devising or found an idea on a Friday morning; she would not mark him down for choosing the wrong subject or failing to touch on certain issues, and though she would have certain expectations according to whether he was known to be charismatic, liturgical or committed to social justice, for the rest she would be open. She was not looking for more information or knowledge; that would have been teaching. She was not looking for guidance or direction and did not expect to be told what to believe or how to behave; that would have approximated to politics or indoctrination. She was not looking for a warm glow inside; that would have bordered on emotionalism. But she did want something that came from beyond and touched her feelings ('made her want . . . ') and at the same time led her to positive action over which she had some control.

Not all theatre does this. Some of it is purely and simply entertainment. But much theatre has something in common with that definition of a good sermon. Theatre at its best is not 'preachy'; once it starts to tell us what we ought to be doing it is in danger of straying into the realms of politics and social engineering. At the same time, it certainly affects our actions. Similarly, it is not didactic. There is no reason to expect that you will know any more when you come out than when you went in, but there is a reasonable expectation that what you do know you will either know more clearly or you will know differently. Your eyes may have been opened wider. You may have been given a different perspective. Whether it actually makes you want to be a better person depends partly on what you have been looking at, but also on you and what you are looking for. However, there is little doubt that your subsequent decisions and actions will be affected by it one way or another.

Not all preachers are aware of this, and some who are aware seem to give it scant attention. Some have been taught that preaching is teaching, will regularly use the preaching spot in the liturgy as a way of giving biblical or doctrinal instruction, and will defend it on the grounds that if they do not teach then, there is no other occasion in the life of the church when they can. Others see preaching as an occasion to comment on events, local, national or international, ecclesiastical or secular, and would like to think they stand in the good Old Testament prophetic tradition, though they know that from time to time they will be charged with preaching their own opinions, with quoting leader writers or commentators from the national press, or accused of trying to influence people. Others again see preaching principally as an occasion to make converts and structure not only sermons but also hymns and prayers to that end.

All these emphases, and many others, are reflected in printed sermons and books on preaching. My concern is not to engage in a critique of such understanding but simply to distinguish others from the one relating to the theatre which I wish to explore more fully. And I begin with the theatre because I want to explore an understanding of preaching more akin to an art form than to a lecture, a political utterance or a piece of evangelical proselytism.

Like the theatre, such a pattern of preaching seeks to present events with which one is familiar and invites the audience to see those events in a new way. Like theatre, it invites the audience to participate, and (still like theatre) what is on offer may be taken by different people at different levels, literally or metaphorically, at face value by one and at some depth by another. Finally, when 'the performance' is over, the audience will not necessarily be expected consciously to act upon it or even to go on thinking about it, though both could be profitable. Those involved in writing and presentation would be gratified if it did. But they would be much happier if they could feel that by that stage something had already happened in the audience, because the purpose of the event is of itself to make something happen, not simply to be the forerunner of something else. In both cases, theatre and preaching, what matters is the act of conception, not foreplay with the possibility of something more to come – maybe! Therefore the task of the preacher, like the playwright, is not so much to *invite* response as to *achieve* response. Hence the title of this book *Preaching as Theatre*.

One reason for this is that the preacher, as Socrates said of himself in the *Theaetetus*, may not be capable personally of bringing forth any fruit of wisdom, but only of acting as 'a spiritual midwife' (as his mother had been a physical one), 'who could enable others to bring to live birth good conceptions with which they were pregnant in the mind, or alternatively help them to recognize an illusory pregnancy and be free of it'.[1]

A second reason is to handle the time-gap between the events of scripture and today. A common request from congregations is that preachers should make more effort to apply, relate or make relevant the scriptures to today, and the best of preachers will attempt to do this. The fact that the request is made is itself evidence of the gap which is felt to exist. But it is also evidence of a felt dis-connection. Congregations feel they are being invited to respond to something that happened in a different time and in a different place, and it is very often when preachers come to make the connection that they become most vulnerable and their audience becomes most challenging. To avoid this pitfall, some preachers choose to begin where their audience is and then turn to the scriptures for enlightenment and instruction, only to find themselves facing the same problem in reverse, because in both cases what we finish up with is a double hermeneutic. First we interpret the Bible and then we try to interpret life in the light of it, bridging the gap as best we can, or we attempt to interpret life by relating it to scripture, often on a highly selective basis.

Jesus and the apostles appear not to have had this problem, though they might have done had they taken the Old Testament as their fundamental frame of reference. Instead, because they firmly addressed the situation as it was, when they preached something happened there and then.[2] People liked it or they didn't like it. They believed it or they didn't believe it. They were made whole or they were not made whole. Incarnation, redemption and judgment were not three events belonging to the past, the present and the future. They were one event belonging to the Now. Jesus did not preach the incarnation by telling us what God had done and then inviting us to believe in it and adjust our lives accordingly. He did it by taking flesh. He did not preach redemption by making people conscious of their sins and then telling them what they had to do to experience forgiveness. He did it by making them feel valued as human beings, whoever they were and whatever they were up to. The urge to 'sin no more' was not a pre-condition or a means of redemption, but the hoped-for (if not the inevitable) response in one to whom something had already happened. Jesus did not preach the resurrection by telling us how it happened and hoping that some would believe. He did it by rising. The preacher's task, therefore, is to reveal the God who is in flesh, to reflect the God who changes lives, and to release the God who is entombed so as to create within the hearers a sense of awareness (if not judgment) of the extent to which they are with the sermon.

A third reason for this approach is that, again like the theatre, it allows for the fact that the listener is not a *tabula rasa*. Listeners come with their own emotions, their own concerns, their own prejudices and interpretations. A woman who is somewhat anxious because her son has just become engaged to a Nigerian and who enters church against the background of an antagonistic father and a bunch of insensitive friends is going to 'hear' any reference to Africa, race, marriage or love quite differently from how she would have heard it a month before, and totally differently from any other member of the congregation that morning. So what worshippers hear is not always (perhaps never) what preachers think they are conveying.

When Clifford Kenyon was MP for Chorley, he related a story of his days as a lay-preacher in the Rossendale Valley when his Socialist politics were well-known and not a little suspect but his Sunday services for the most part were much appreciated. However, finding himself on one occasion preaching shortly before a national election at one of the more 'upper crust' churches in the Valley, wisdom dictated that he play safe, and he took a fairly innocuous Bible study-type sermon which any preacher might use for a theological sermon class. Six months later they invited him back, by which time the election was well out of everybody's mind and he felt the freedom to return to type. When the service was over one of the old deacons came forward and greeted him at the bottom of the pulpit steps. 'Ay,' he said, in his Lancashire way, 'that were a grand sermon, lad . . . it really were, and there's a lot of folk here this morning saying so. You were a lot better 'an when you come last time . . . 'cos last time, you know, you tended to be a bit political!' 'The politics,' said Kenyon, 'are often not so much in the preacher as in the listener.'

At times this can be disastrous. They attack you afterwards for things you never said, intended to say or even thought of. But at other times it can be creative, can introduce a timeless quality to the sermon, and may even help to bridge the time gap I referred to earlier.

In 1995 the Minerva Theatre in Chichester revived Harold Pinter's *The Hothouse*, a play first performed in 1958, set in an institution almost anywhere in England and relating to power, authority and bureaucracy. The play was the same play. The audience was totally different. In 1958 we were in the days of Orwell, when power and authority took you in a straight line to Big Brother, institutional life was just recovering from the dark days of the war, and all kinds of new local authority and more caring 'homes' were coming into being. In 1995 we were in the days of closing homes and institutions in favour of community care, when cults were exercising a new authority over many of their members, when the Conservative government was in a state of collapse alongside many traditional institutions which seemed to be dying. The setting inevitably changed the meaning of so many lines, and the warden's Christmas Day message to the residents towards the end sounded incredibly like the Queen on Christmas Day or the Prime Minister trying to gee-up a flagging nation. Something similar can happen in the sermon, so that what the worshippers hear, in relation to where they are already, may often give them new and sometimes profound insight – and on occasions, the Word of God.

There is a fourth reason for this approach. It makes it more difficult for the listener to escape. As long as we stay in the realm of ideas with all our twentieth-century Western assumptions and appurtenances we shall also be well-equipped to reject whatever it is the preacher chooses to hold up before us. Try shifting the ground from the ideas and the mind to the feelings and the heart, to identification with what it is we are seeing, and our defences are down. And it is when our defences are down that God has his opportunity.

Frederick Franck[3] tells how in a 'Seeing and Drawing' workshop, in which at least one student could not even draw a straight line, he asked his students to let their eyes fall on one thing in front of them – a leaf, a bush, a tree. They were then to close their eyes for five minutes, after which they were to open them and focus on whatever they observed before. They were to

> look it in the eye, until you feel it looking back at you. Feel that you are alone with it on Earth! That it is the most important thing in the universe, that it contains all the riddles of life and death. It does! *You are no longer looking, you are SEEING* . . . (capitals his, italics mine.)

They were told not to feel they were being 'creative'; they were just doing 'an experiment in seeing'.

From here Franck goes on to show[4] how so much time in the twentieth century is spent looking – lenses, telescopes, television tubes! 'Never has it been more urgent to speak of seeing.' We become onlookers and spectactors, subjects who look at objects. We stick labels on things. We kick things we have barely perceived.

Looking and seeing both start with sense perception, but there the similarity ends. When I 'look' at the world and label its phenomena, I make immediate choices, instant appraisals – I like or I dislike, I accept or I reject, what I look at, according to its usefulness to the 'Me' . . . THIS IS THE ME THAT I IMAGINE MYSELF TO BE, and that I try to impose on others.

The purpose of 'looking' is to survive, to cope, to manipulate, to discern what is useful, agreeable, or threatening to the Me, what enhances or what diminishes the Me. This we are trained to do from our first day.

When, on the other hand, I SEE – suddenly I am all eyes, I forget the Me, am liberated from it and dive into the reality of what confronts me, become part of it, participate in it. I no longer label, no longer choose.

Franck then goes on to expound Zen, not as something exotically oriental, a fad or a Buddhist sect, but as being in touch with the inner workings of life, 'the moment speaking as time and as eternity'. Preachers who can help their listeners to 'see' rather than to 'look' are much more likely to find something happening even before they have reached the church porch at the end of the service. Worshippers who find themselves responding at depths and with talents that they did not even know they had will thank them for it, though not always at the time. They are 'beginning to draw', though they may not fully appreciate what has happened for some years to come.

As long as preaching is seen as lecturing or teaching, then, in order for it to be effective, listeners have to go away and do something about it. If it is art, they don't. By the time it is over something has happened, or has failed to happen. This is what makes preaching as an art distinctive, more exciting and satisfying when it works, more depressing and worrying when it doesn't. Those who have attempted it know well what Wordsworth experienced when he wrote,

Whither is fled the visionary gleam?
Where is it now, the glory and the dream?[5]

But then in a poem written because he felt he had lost for ever the presence of the Muse or the secret of his craft, he amply demonstrates that it is there all the time.

So what is this art? It is better to illustrate than to define, and that is therefore what I propose to do. Afterwards, in Chapter 5, will be the time to distinguish it from the more familiar and traditional understanding of preaching as teaching, to relate it to other calls for change in preaching currently emerging in one or two places, and to reflect on how it chimes in with recent trends in contemporary biblical interpretation.

I

Beginning with the Bible

Preachers from a biblical tradition will have a strong feeling that whatever they do must be biblically related. Not for them political comment such as you may find in the leader columns of the more serious daily papers, nor trite remarks or homilies derived from personal experience, fleshed out with a few biblical anecdotes or illustrated by Bible stories. A sermon *may* have a title, but it *must* have a text, or at least a passage of scripture which will be all-pervading, in theory if not always in practice. Eisegesis may too often take precedence over exegesis, but only by default or lack of recognition. Opening the Bible and expounding the scriptures is what it is all about. For congregations in the same tradition the test of a sermon will be whether what the preacher said is a fair interpretation of the text or at least can be substantiated by reference to other parts of the sacred text. Any talk about 'making something happen' therefore will only be entertained if that 'something' can pass the same test. For this reason we begin with the Bible.

The size of the Bible and the wide variety of genres to be found there inevitably call for selection, and I propose to pay particular attention to the prophets and the use of stories.

The prophetic tradition

Why the prophets?

Apart from the obvious reason that they are the natural starting point for anything on prophetic preaching, the prophets form the second major section of the Old Testament (second only to the Torah) and focus within themselves a number of different traditions. There are considerable differences, for example, between the prophets and seers of the historical books, the eighth-century (or writing) prophets, the major prophets and the minor prophets (or Book of the Twelve), but taken together they represent what can well be described as a prophetic tradition. Moreover, though they feature less conspicuously (and indeed differently again) in the New Testament, there can be no doubt that much of the prophetic tradition is taken for granted there and underlies the ministry of Jesus and the life and work of the early church.

A second reason is that the very variations that emerged in the activity of the prophets over a period of a thousand years are an indication of their adaptability.[1] Unlike the Torah, which had great difficulty adapting, the prophets seem to have found little, if any, difficulty adapting not so much their message as their method in order to make their points. So the preacher who sees himself in this tradition ought not to have too much difficulty in adapting either.

Third, the prophetic tradition embodies a useful mix of 'the now' and 'the always'. The utterances of the prophets have a certain specificity about them. They arise in a given situation and are directly related to it. A year later, ten years later, they could not have said what they did, or they would have had to say it differently. Old sermons, summer re-runs and Sunday evening repeats after a gap of five years are not on! Fully to appreciate the prophets and understand what they were driving at therefore calls for study and research, often involving information now no longer accessible, and therefore the prophetic word as originally intended is denied us.

Yet, at the same time, the words of the prophets have a timeless quality about them, in two respects. On the one hand, with a little imagination it is possible to enter into their situation, to imagine the problem they were handling, what they were doing with it and how their hearers would react to it, in such a way as to feel a common bond between their day and ours. And on the other hand, a reading of the prophets suggests that at its heart the message they are dealing with is one that is relevant to every generation in every time and place. What is said and what happens may differ considerably, but the underlying issues, both human and divine, never go away, and change little, if at all. At some points they may require the preacher to do a lot of homework in order to get inside the biblical material and make it come alive, yet at another level, particularly in the narratives, a little imagination may work wonders. Perhaps nowhere more than in the prophets is it possible to go in and out of the text or to move back and forth between past and present.[2]

Fourth, like all good theatre, the words of the prophets can be taken at different levels. They can even mean different things to different people. They are stories to one, politics to another, and for this reason they provide a useful introduction to some of the other material we shall be looking at later.

Fifth, the varied interpretations now coming through to us from the Third World, the feminists and so on, as we shall see later,[3] are themselves a good example of the prophetic tradition at work. They both open up the possibility of our doing something similar and at the same time provide us with some of the raw material to do it.

But the last and by far more important reason for beginning here is that it is the prophets who were doing in their day exactly what I am suggesting needs to be done in ours: making something happen, and at different levels. At one level the prophets expect somebody, be he king or commoner, to hear what they say and to take note (the Word), but they expect the hearer also to do more than 'take note' – they expect to see something happen almost at once (the deed).[4] Where that fails, they engage in acts of prophetic symbolism which are more than dramatic gestures – they are intended not only to proclaim something but actually to set in motion or to bring about what they proclaim.

The effect of this is twofold. On the one hand it is meant to do something to the person whose regular communications may not come through the ears or the mind but through the heart and the gut. If the hearers are not responding, let us touch them in a different part of their anatomy. But then, on the other hand, since in the Hebrew psyche the point of prophetic symbolism was to make something happen of itself, this symbolism was meant also to achieve something over and above the hearer's will and inbuilt powers of resistance.

That is why I say that the prophets' method is my method. They illustrate what I am writing about by doing it. It is not, however, my intention to present a case for prophetic preaching today (that is, 'making something happen') on the strength of the prophetic tradition, but rather to see whether by exploring that tradition we may enrich our own.

Who wants a prophet?

Probably the short answer is 'nobody', especially if you take the trouble to explain that what we understand by prophecy is not 'foretelling' but 'forthtelling'.[5] But do we *need* a prophet? Most people would probably still say not. Prophets can never expect to be popular or greatly in demand. They never have been. Prophetic preaching is never 'the flavour of the month', and when it is, the prophets themselves need to be worried about it. Part of the problem is the image: it suggests austerity, puritanism, awkwardness, disagreement, minorities and the like. But a bigger problem is the message; it frightens people.

Preachers, therefore, who decide to develop this line must expect to begin (and will probably have to continue) with a steady campaign to justify what they are doing to the point where even those who dislike it or would dismiss it nevertheless have to admit that, both in the church and in society at large, we do need people like the prophet around. How? Like the prophets, not by arguing about it but by doing it, and by drawing on the 250 years of intense creative prophetic activity to explore the variety that is there, so as to provide the variety that we need. There are levels of understanding as well as attack. Here are four examples.

The fairy story
Hans Christian Andersen's tale of 'The Emperor's New Clothes' is a good example of the Old Testament prophet, because the prophet does what the child did. It could be used simply as a prologue in any service of worship where this facet of prophecy was to be considered and the significant features brought out then or later.

First, that child saw clearly what other people were all confused about and said what many people really knew was true but never had the courage to admit. Why? They were concerned for their reputation, and the child didn't know what a reputation was. Secondly, he spoke the truth, simply and directly, in a situation where nobody wanted to hear it. The emperor didn't want to hear it because he had been led to believe he was wearing the finest suit there was – that was the power of the tailor's advertising, promotion and marketing procedures. The tailor didn't want to hear it because exposure of that kind meant the end of his business. And the people didn't want to hear it because they had been conned into believing that if they didn't just say 'Yes' to what they were being told (or 'sold') there must be something the matter with *them*. Third, therefore, if the truth were to be spoken in that situation, it needed someone who had missed out on all the promotion and was out of touch with what was going on, or who knew he was on to a loser but had nothing to lose, or who had not been sufficiently 'programmed' to keep his mouth shut, because these are the camps from which the prophets came.

Already it may be becoming a little clearer why we need prophets. Indeed, in that form they might almost begin to be attractive. Stay with the child and in the form of a fairy story and we feel safe. We can dismiss it. It only becomes disturbing as we come nearer to reality.

It might be helpful, therefore, to give listeners a chance to participate, preferably in silence! Invite them to name *their* prophet. Who for them today is doing what that child did? And if they cannot think of names, can they think of types? Is it a royal, a politican, a media figure, a newspaper writer, a dramatist, a novelist, an interviewer or a poet? On the spur of the moment they are not going to make a final judgment, but they can be encouraged simply to take the name that comes to the top of their head in the light of what they have just heard. It will give them a backcloth against which to make judgments on our second example.

The biblical prophet

There are two classic stories of this kind of activity in the early days of the prophetic movement. Both concern rulers who overstep their authority or take advantage of their position, though the underlying principles apply just as much to everyone else, and both demonstrate very effectively the power of the prophet to achieve a result. One is the story of Nathan over David and Bathsheba and the other the story of Elijah over Naboth's vineyard.[6] Since we shall be dealing with the second later,[7] we shall confine our attention here to the first.

Of all the stories of the prophets, the Nathan story is perhaps one of the most uncomplicated illustrations of what I have in mind. It would indeed be hard to find a better way of making something happen in the heart of the king than to tell the story of the poor man with his ewe lamb. Of course David would feel he had been got at, and in a sense he had. He had so beautifully been led up the garden path. But it was not Nathan who had got at him. David had got at himself. Give him the facts plainly and simply, and he had no doubt what he ought to do. His difficulty was relating those facts to himself under the pressures of daily living. That he was led up the garden path so easily, with no idea what Nathan was getting at and not the slightest smelling of a rat, is itself an indication of the utter insensitivity of the man at this point. Yet nothing else would have moved him. Hortatory utterances (oughts and shoulds) would have put him on the defensive and might have brought the prophet a 'rich reward' for his pains. Logical arguments on moral grounds could have been met with counter-arguments. Whereas all Nathan does is to relate a carefully planned anecdote which gets under David's skin and creates an inner conviction. The story is enough.[8] Preachers who want to preach judgment, take note! And the story is open enough to admit choice. Once David hears the message, he has a choice as to whether he acknowledges it or suppresses it. Preachers who want to preach for decision, take note!

For all these reasons, this story may be regarded as the prototype of the sort of prophetic activity that makes things happen. It has all the attributes of the child in 'The Emperor's New Clothes', except that in this case the prophet knew exactly what he was doing. This is why we need prophets, and not only in pulpits – people who cannot be controlled by censorship and who themselves will do all they can to resist the censorship of others.

The Old Testament prophet fundamentally was one whom nobody could silence. Today, of course, he can be dismissed. He is long ago and far away. But what happens if you bring him (or her) nearer? What happens when you suddenly spot your 'biblical prophet' still doing the rounds?

Rick Gibson[9] is a serious collector of human organs and tissues for the purposes of art. Because they are difficult to come by and yet many people have them, he decided to walk through Reading carrying a placard saying what he wanted. He negotiated with the police, who warned him that though it would be offensive to many people and he might run into trouble, what he was doing was legal and they had no reason to stop him. In the event everything passed off quite well. Two weeks later he decided to try the same thing in Brighton, only to be met at the railway station by the police. They told him to return immediately to London because if he set one foot out of the station he would be arrested. Feeling his basic rights were being threatened, he disobeyed and spent the rest of the day in a Brighton cell. What puzzled Gibson, as a Canadian, was that the law was one thing in Brighton and another in Reading.

> 'When I look back on my six years in England,' he wrote afterwards, 'I realize that I learnt to despise a legal system based on inaccessible, unwritten laws. This is the stuff of Third World countries where powerful élites dominate ignorant masses who are unable to defend themselves against oddly flexible laws. Most modern democracies have dealt with this type of tyranny by creating a constitution with a charter of rights and freedoms and a criminal code.'

The obvious question is whether we need a prophet to tell us that our case law and British legal system and criminal code are not really all we like to think they are, but maybe that is so obvious that we would not need to ask it. The story has done its job.

Once we get nearer to home, we also begin to see why the prophet is so unpopular. He frightens us. Here is one who fearlessly deals in truth at a level we do not normally penetrate, and though we have no idea where it will lead, something inside tells us it will be there long after we have gone. After that there is little more to be said. Something has happened.

At this point it may be appropriate to ask congregations to recall the prophet they first thought of. How does that prophet stand up in the light of what I have just said? Seasoned churchgoers, of course, will have their defences. 'All very interesting,' they will say, 'but of course our situation is so different from that of Nathan.' So this may be the point to move on to some of the eighth-century prophets whose approach is different and who need different treatment.

The modern prophet

A modern prophet is someone who is saying what the biblical prophets said, but in a contemporary situation about which we all care. It may be the preacher himself, a radio or television commentator or programme, or a newspaper columnist.[10]

Here are some extracts from a newspaper columnist from the time when Norman Lamont was under attack as Chancellor of the Exchequer on account of allegations against his personal life. This was a period when there was much unrest in the country about the willingness of politicians to take responsibility for their actions, the quality of public life, and what it takes to make a political figure resign:[11]

> It's all getting a touch like Macbeth, the bit where he's committed so much murder and mayhem his senses have become numbed and dreadful deeds no longer startle him. We've supp'd full with scandals these last few months and weeks . . . So the Report published this week . . . on the affair of Norman Lamont, his sex-therapist tenant and Peter Carter-Ruck's legal fees hasn't achieved quite the impact it might have had in a more innocent era.
>
> Not surprising; it's had some stiff competition recently. BCCI and Robert Maxwell, swindling ordinary people out of millions; Matrix-Churchill . . . the illegality of the pit closure programme. Another day, another scandal.
>
> Official deceit, disinformation and dissembling are now so routine they barely merit comment . . . This has become a society with no rules . . . Scarcely anyone ever takes responsi-

bility for anything. Accountability is becoming a fossilized concept.

If the abbreviated version is severe, it is even more severe in its entirety, and would certainly make most congregations sit up and take notice. For some it would cut deep. But of course it is open to objection on the grounds that it is only one person's opinion. Not everyone likes this prophet, and not everything she writes is prophetic, both criticisms which could have been made of all the prophets. Some would even object to such 'readings' in church.

But what happens when the contemporary and the biblical are put side by side and seem to be saying the same thing? Before anyone can walk out, try putting that kind of contemporary comment alongside similar words from one of the prophets, such as Amos 2. 6–8; 4. 1–3; 5. 11–12 or 6. 4–7.[12]

Perhaps the time has come to remind the congregation again of the prophets they first thought of. How do these prophets look now? Can they think of a few more? Or should the preacher help them by suggesting one or two whom he or she has spotted?

The eighth-century prophets

By the time we get to the eighth century, with Isaiah 1–39 and several of the minor prophets, prophecy has become somewhat more sophisticated. In general there is less of the personal encounter, the anecdote and the isolated incident and more about social conditions, rich and poor, treaties and alliances, rulers and politics. The king and the court are not so much individuals as part of an increasingly powerful social structure. The *ordinary* people are exactly that and increasingly made to feel it,[13] and preachers who want to move to and fro between the text and our situation,[14] provided they are prepared to do their homework, will find themselves increasingly living in two worlds not all that far apart.

We will take two examples, in each case suggesting themes which arise within the prophets but are expressed in more familiar contemporary terminology, so as to help the listener to move between the two worlds. In other days other themes and other language may be more appropriate, but much of the background would apply equally well to other prophets operating in the same time and place.

(i) Hosea: whatever happened to traditional values?[15]

The title will immediately ring bells. One may begin by describing Hosea's situation as far as possible in language which reflects our own and which at points may evoke our world rather than his world, so that the congregation may have to pause to think which world we are talking about. For example:

> Our story this morning is about a nation which had known better days but had fallen on hard times and was having difficulty making the adjustment.
>
> Compared to the great civilizations of the ancient world this nation was relatively young – its folk history went back close on 1000 years, but it had really only existed as a unity for about half that time, and its heyday was no more than 100–200 years in the past. Compared to other nations it was also very small, both geographically and numerically. There were those around who often wondered how it ever managed to achieve the position that it had, and there were not a few cynics who wondered whether it really did have any position at all except in the minds of those who belonged to it.
>
> It was very much a nation in two parts. In its heyday the drive and the wealth-creation was in the North, but in more recent times the North had virtually collapsed and the South was trying desperately to save itself and to work out a future on its own.
>
> There were also problems with the monarchy. In the good old days they had good old kings – reliable, respected leaders. (They didn't really, but they thought they had!) More recently royalty didn't seem to have what it took and could never quite get it right, and there were even those around who not only challenged what royals did but actually questioned whether they were needed at all.
>
> That was Israel in the eighth century BC, and on to the stage steps a man called Hosea with a message from God.

The picture is now clear. We are in the Bible. But our own world is not far away. So what has this prophet to say? First, he had to tell the people what they were doing wrong. A careful choice of words can keep the parallel going:

One, *they had lost the customary virtues of community life.* Judges, for example, were not behaving as you would expect judges to behave: they were no longer 100% trustworthy and were not averse to the occasional bribe. People's feelings were similar to those of many today about the British legal system, and not only the legal system. People have feelings about clergy: you don't expect clergy to have secret assignations, and if they do and they are caught, you at least expect them to come clean and not lie about it. The same goes for doctors: affairs may be allowed – that's up to them – but not with clients. After all, these people were chosen for the job and put there in the first place because they were thought to be reliable and above this sort of thing.

Two, there seemed to be *an unwillingness on the part of society to respond generously with help to a fellow human being who was in need,* such as a member of the family who had fallen on hard times. Earlier in the nation's history, when David had run through most of his exploits and began to realize that he had been a bit of a bastard, he sent out a message to see if there was anything he could do to make amends. He was referred to Mephibosheth, the lame son of his old friend Jonathan. He invited Mephibosheth to live in the palace and eat at his table, and he gave him lands. Of course, it could be argued that he had a bad conscience, and critics say that he was only returning to Mephibosheth what he had taken from him in the first place. However, Hosea's concern is that now not even that seems to apply any longer. And it is not only royalty but also the *nouveau riche* who no longer seem to have any sense that, having taken so much out of the community, they have a responsibility to put some of it back. Instead, they just walk off with it for themselves and their heirs.

Three, *idolatry is everywhere.* People are dominated by false and foreign gods. Idolatry in biblical terms is not just images and icons in church or arguments about world religions in the schools. It's the worship of false gods: money as it is worshipped in the City, power as it is worshipped in many new and rapidly growing forms of management, indifference as it is worshipped in local democracy, and sycophancy as it is worshipped in the police force and many of our older British institutions.

With idolatry go *sacrifice and ritual rather than real and meaningful loving relationships*. Still a problem. Witness the way . . .

What is happening here is not a criticism of the British situation. We are still firmly describing Hosea's world, but we are using the current situation to help us to feel our way into Hosea's message, not using Hosea to make comments on Britain.

For Hosea, the people's most serious offence was that they *were forgetting where they had come from*. They must remember they had come from nowhere. Less than 1000 years ago they were slaves. Less than 500 years ago they were a loose collection of tribes. Yet they were talking as if they were one of the great powers of the world, and all because of their own efforts. 'Knowledge of God' (Hosea's phrase for what is lacking, or for traditional values maybe) means first acknowledging that no nation has anything of right. Anything and everything is a gift from God.

A nation with a high standard of democracy, a good legal system and a criminal justice system must always see that as a gift from God and not as something it has achieved through its own brilliance. A nation which claims to be the defender of the free world must see that position as a gift from God and not as something it has achieved by virtue of its financial resources, its arms or its loud voice. And a nation which attributes its former greatness to its empire must seriously consider whether that empire was truly a gift from God or whether it might have come from its own vandalism or greedy grasping.

By now listeners may be forgiven for again being unsure whether we are in Hosea's world or in our world. But is there much difference? Of course they may mis-hear and think that the preacher is really using Hosea to have a bash at a few Aunt Sallies, but if the preacher is careful about the biblical background and ensures that the language is factual and descriptive rather than critical, the congregation will slowly learn to respect his or her integrity. However, what they are looking for is something positive. What has Hosea got to offer? Two points.

First, *Hosea rarely if ever goes for individuals.* He goes for society. He neither personalizes nor trivializes, and his politics are not royal politics or party politics but people politics, because in the last resort it is we and not they who are responsible for the society to which we belong. Slowly, by now, the ground is shifting. We are becoming less objective and descriptive. We are no longer pointing the finger out there. Somebody is bringing on the mirror, and, as with David and Mephibosheth, the re-creation of that society has something to do with the divisions in our society and the way we feel about one another. Officers and men in the forces. Management and unions in industry. Women in a man's world. And so on.

But this is no longer only *Hosea's* world. Our world is taking over. There is a contemporary ring to it. This means that when I feel resentful about the costs of the Health Service because I scarcely use it, or of the schools because either I never had any children or they are grown up, or of leisure centres, parks and pools because I don't need them, or of the care of the elderly because though I am old I have always managed to look after myself, I am in fact all the time making a massive statement about myself, my view of other people and the world I belong to. John Donne was on target when he said 'No man is an island';[16] not only in the negative sense that 'another man's death diminishes me', but also in the positive sense that another man's life depends on me. This was Hosea's concern. He was worried by a nation which found God when it was in slavery but lost God when it was delivered.

Second, Hosea (like many of us) had great *difficulty making up his mind whether things had always been like that or whether in more recent days they had got worse.* He swings between the two. But what he *is* clear about is that however bad things were, there *was always the possibility of reform* and of finding a true greatness based on the continued love of God, provided that people were willing to pay the price. For there was no way God could give up the nation he had chosen, any more than parents can cast off the child they have brought to birth. The price was repentance and suffering.

To avoid reverting to 'preaching as telling' at this point, it may help to change the scene once more so as to re-establish contact with the feelings and to conclude with a concrete example from another culture, also having problems with knowledge of God and traditional values: Germany 1942, through the eyes of Bonhoeffer.

Less than a century before, Germany had been a loose collection of states prior to unification under Bismarck. Like Israel it had risen from nothing, and in spite of the horrors of the First World War had reached a position where it could dominate Europe, extend its influence to North Africa and the Far East, and claim to be the defender of the true faith and the Aryan races for the benefit of the world.

Bonhoeffer was one of those Germans – straight out of the top drawer of German society, and as far from Nazism as you could get. Yet in 1942 he was feeling such a deep sense of responsibility for what was happening that he was prepared to go to the point of risking his neck (and eventually losing it) in an attempt to bring peace between Britain and Germany in a plot which back-fired and was interpreted as treachery. Hosea would have liked Bonhoeffer – because Bonhoeffer was saying that there is something more important than German ascendancy, something more important than trying to re-create a past, and something more important than Hitler and Nazism. What both Bonhoeffer and Hosea want us to feel is that true greatness which comes only through suffering and which leads us to an increasing awareness of the source of our strength. This is Hosea's 'knowledge of God'.

Like Bonhoeffer, what Hosea preached he practised. I referred earlier to prophetic symbolism. So it was that Hosea had actually married a prostitute called Gomer. It's not clear whether he married a prostitute to demonstrate that if he could love and give himself to her so Yahweh would commit himself to Israel – or whether he married a good woman who became a prostitute to bring home to Israel how Israel had treated Yahweh and then stayed loyal to Gomer to demonstrate how Yahweh would stay loyal to Israel. But in both cases the message for the future is the same. Whatever Israel had done, Yahweh would never cast her off.

By now, if the preacher has done the job well, the congregation should be identifying and feeling with two men who brought hope to a desperate situation and who cared enough to go to the extent of personal involvement, suffering and sacrifice, and neither situation so very different from our own. All that is needed is that one sentence which focuses the issue on which the listeners must make a decision. The sermon could end like this:

> (Whatever Israel had done Yahweh would never cast her off.) But Israel could only know that in its bones when, like Bonhoeffer and Germany, like Hosea and Gomer, Israel had learned to drink that cup of suffering.
> The question for us is 'Can we?'

(ii) Micah: the voice of the voiceless

When certain sections of society start helping themselves at the expense of the weak and powerless, that might just be the moment to look at Micah in terms of 'the voice of the voiceless'. The obvious text is Micah 6. 8, well-worn and disarmingly simple, indicating to the congregation that three points are on their way and that they are unlikely to disagree with them. But does it have to be like that? Could we perhaps hear a different message, or the same message differently, if only we could hear it in a different context?

Suppose, for example, we begin with Micah not as a figure of the Establishment, calling people to do what is so obviously right, but as an early-day liberation theologian,[17] challenging what the Establishment was up to. That may not put the cat among the pigeons right away, but at least it's enough for one or two pigeons to show signs of agitation. 'How was Micah a liberation theologian?', they ask.

Well, he was *in* the world but not *of* the world – literally and geographically! He was near enough to the hub of activity in Jerusalem to know what was going on there – what was

happening in the temple and among the priests; what was
happening in the court and among the rulers and 'politicians',
and what was happening to the mass of people who were
dependent on what was happening but had no share in it. At the
same time he himself lived about twenty-five miles outside
Jerusalem. Just far enough to commute by day and to brush it off
by night. He didn't need to get involved. He might be forgiven for
not even noticing. But in Micah's case it was this very distancing
of himself from it all, coupled with an acute sensitivity and
concern, which gave him his unique (and often unpopular) view.

Of Micah as a person we know very little. One view is that he
was a small farmer who wanted to protect his own interests along
with those of his equals. Another is that he was a person of some
substance who somehow had stumbled on the poor as the victims
of injustice and believed 'enough was enough'. A third view is
that he was a theologian who had thrown in his lot with the
oppressed and become a fearless defender of their human rights.
Any one of these views would have been enough to earn him the
title of a liberation theologian. Living in an evil world, he saw
things from the divine perspective.

What did he see? After a long period of stability and steady
growth he saw things beginning to fall apart. In a thousand years
his people had moved from insignificance and ignominious
slavery, a tiny nation in a small world, to become a nation with a
king, a court, a temple and a faith. They had seen the northern
kingdom destroyed, but the South was holding up well and was
thought to be indestructible. Only in the last forty or fifty years
had things there started to go downhill. The king, in desperation,
had dared to talk of alliances with foreign powers (like Assyria)
for protection, and one result was that foreigners were extracting
tributes, with the burden always falling on the poor. Problems of
the economy did not just arrive in the late twentieth century!

Micah saw changes taking place in land ownership. For the
Israelites, an agricultural community from earliest times, land
had always been important. In the early days of the settlement
they had to take what they could, and naturally some did better
than others. However, for the most part they fought it out 'on a
level playing field'. But come the monarchy, and the growth of a

rich élite that went with it, land in the fertile valleys became more desirable than land on the hillside. Powerful people had the opportunity to take it, and they did. Small landowners lost ground to big landowners. The weak began to go to the wall.

Better land then meant better living. The discovery of iron meant better tools for those who could afford them. Better tools meant better results. Better results meant more money. More money saw the beginnings of a market in luxury goods. All of which could have been so wonderful because everybody could have benefited from the prosperity. Instead, those who had wealth kept it for themselves and then to their selfishness added corruption. Increasingly, the powerful took the fields, then the homes, then the women and the children for slaves.

The powers-that-be could, of course, have done something about it. They could have regulated the abuses, even if they couldn't have stopped them altogether. They did not. Instead, they joined in. Micah says that they treated people as if they were sheep for slaughter (3.1), and what inflamed him most of all was that it was not just the king and the rulers but also the judiciary and many of the prophets who were parties to the injustice and gave no sign whatsoever of 'biting the hand that fed them'. Yet the change was so gradual and so subtle that the only people who seemed to notice were the victims, and they were the last group who could do anything about it. That was what Micah saw that made him a liberation theologian.

If we have difficulty with this idea, perhaps it is because we are less aware than we might be of the injustices of the society we are living in. Examples should not be too difficult to find, but personal impressions which cannot be gainsaid may be more effective than issues which could only initiate long debates. I thought I knew all about 'banana republics', for example, until I travelled through Costa Rica (by no means one of the worst examples) shortly before an election and saw the various political colours outside the houses and farms. 'Not necessarily the political parties those people support', said my driver, 'but the ones they will vote for – they vote with their landlord!' I thought I knew about the struggle for justice in Eastern Europe until I read Kafka's novel *The Trial* and felt the resonance way beyond

Czechoslovakia in the early twentieth century. I thought I knew about the evils of *apartheid* until I realized that until a few years ago Desmond Tutu didn't have a vote. Then I thought all these injustices belonged to other nations, until I looked in a mirror!

So what did Micah say to all this? It wasn't so much what he said as what he did, and Itumeleng Mosala, who teaches Religious Studies in Cape Town, coming to Micah through the eyes of South Africa, sees two things often overlooked.

First, before ever he became a voice for the voiceless, Micah joined the voiceless. Solidarity! That way he began to see as they saw. Perhaps it helps if we can paint a picture of how everything looks different when we see the world from a wheel chair, or (literally crawling on our hands and knees) with the eye of a child, or through Micah's tears (1. 8–9), which Mosala sees as a genuine expression of solidarity and the first step towards liberation.

Secondly, the heart of Micah's message was revolutionary. Living in South Africa leads Mosala to feel there is more to 'swords into ploughshares' (4. 3–4) than we might imagine from the peace movement. True, Micah is 'anti-swords', but not simply because of violence and killing; he believes defence and war are wrong because they are always a luxury for the few: to preserve power for the rulers, the middle classes and those who benefit from it. What interests him much more is 'pro-ploughshares', where the emphasis is on something for everybody. His is a summons to put first things first: food, the economy and survival. Here are the beginnings of true people power with something special for those who need it most: a liberating word from a liberation theologian.

Looked at like that, doing justly, loving loyalty and walking humbly is no longer something we are told we ought to do, like a new commandment. It is an invitation to share a way of life, or a covenant written on the heart, and only the heart can respond.

In the end, hopefully one has avoided the Scylla of saying something trite and well-worn about traditional values or solidarity bolstered by a few relevant texts or Bible stories and the Charybdis of saying something scholarly or historical about Hosea or Micah plus a few relevant words for today. The test is whether the congregation is drawn into either story in such a way that they begin to feel that it is *their* story.

Bible stories

Bible stories follow naturally from a consideration of the prophetic tradition because they form a major part of the Bible, especially in the Old Testament but also in the Gospels and Acts. They are interesting and often arresting, easy to remember and, because they can be taken at more than one level, open up many possibilities. One person can take them straight, another can explore them further, and a third can spot something of personal value which others will never even notice. Stories rely less on background knowledge than is the case with the prophets, offer scope for an imaginative preacher to plumb the depths, and make it possible even for 'simple' people to perceive the depths being plumbed.[18]

Like the prophets, Bible stories demonstrate what I am talking about, in that they too have a capacity to make things happen. If they are told so as to bring out the nuances and shades of understanding which are clearly there but may not be immediately apparent, with skilful use of words and phrases which strike chords because the hearer is familiar with the language in a different context, they also can enable two worlds to come together and speak to each other so that the hearer moves from one to the other and the preacher's message is completed in the mind and heart of the listener.

Here are three examples. The first shows what can be done when you take a familiar story and offer more than one identification for the *dramatis personae* so that the congregation can determine for themselves the setting in which they wish to view the drama and see what happens, as the words of the preacher at times chime in with their perception, at other times jar with their perception, and on occasions very nearly throw them off course altogether.

The second shows what can happen when you take a familiar story, with a precise identification of *dramatis personae*, but then interpret it alongside a piece of Filipino peasant thinking,[19] less linear and literalistic than Western Protestantism, in such a way as to shed light on personal relationships within the family and between First and Third Worlds, on the biblical narrative and on our own human situation.

The third shows what can happen when you take a familiar incident with a number of exegetical and homiletical problems and put it down in a different, preferably unfamiliar, context which seems light years away from it.

'The Tale of the Chariot Wheel'

'The Tale of the Chariot Wheel' took its rise in the late 1980s when Thatcherism was still stalking the land and people in all walks of life, not least in the big institutions of health, education and civil service, which had always had a high degree of professionalism and personal commitment, were feeling threatened and devalued.[20]

'The Tale of the Chariot Wheel' (or 'Mount Carmel and the Chariot Chase')[21] is a tale of three: Jezebel, Ahab and Elijah. However, whether they are three people, three families, three nations or three institutions the hearer may be left to judge. First, the characters.

Begin with Jezebel, described in one Bible dictionary[22] as 'ruthless' in character, with a 'lust for power', 'unshrinking and resolute' in all her activities, and 'remorseless' in her 'brushing aside of anything and everything that interfered with the carrying out of her designs'. The name means 'unwanted', which may have something to do with it. (Even by this stage it would have been hard for the congregation not to be thinking of someone else!)

Living with the Jews, Jezebel's problem is that she is not 'one of them', and as far as she is concerned Ahab and his people can never be 'one of us'. Yet she knows that Ahab's people are the real people of power. They always had been. They are special – chosen – and they know it. Their roots go right back into history. Jezebel has had a different kind of upbringing. Her people were traders. In a way – in her own way – she has done very well. She may have belonged to an inferior race, but she has got sufficiently high up the tree to marry into the aristocracy and claim her rights.

In Jezebel's book, the trouble with the Jews was not so much that they were a people of power but that they were in a rut. Because they had never really had to fight for what they had, they had become slack. Decadent! What their society needed was a good shake-up. Even this god, their Yahweh, was not a patch on the god she had inherited from her fathers. So what better than to introduce her own brand of religion, and where better to begin than with her husband and his cronies?

Ahab is a different kind of character. He represents the Establishment – not the religious Establishment particularly, but just the Establishment, though in his case there wasn't much difference. Like all kings and queens, he takes his position for granted rather more than he takes it seriously. Being king is how it is. The world is how it is. You have to take it as it is. You may move a piece of furniture here, another piece there, but if you are king the one thing you don't do is ask questions, or you may discover that your position is untenable. Your job is to preserve stability, and if you can use religion to help, to silence the prophets or to persuade them to be content with inanities, so much the better.

In any circumstances, a marriage like that was going to be stormy. What neither of them had reckoned with was the forcefulness of Elijah.

Elijah is different again. His origins are irrelevant. His power resides neither in his ancestry nor in a long list of personal achievements, but entirely in the truth of what he says. If he appears to be a nutcase, then the people will dismiss him as a nutcase. If what he says resonates with them, then they will claim him as God's man. And on this occasion that is precisely what happens. They may not rush madly after him like a charismatic figure, for after all kings are kings and you do have to consider your family and their safety, your person and your mortage, but deep down everybody knows that what Elijah is saying makes sense.

Ahab, in his saner moments, probably agrees. Indeed, when Jezebel is not listening, he says as much. He probably quite likes Elijah really – if only he would not rock the boat. And Elijah probably quite likes Ahab – he's the sort of person you can make a friend of. Kings and 'prophets' have lived like this in healthy, creative tension for centuries. It suits both parties. Kings know that the right kind of religious challenge is good for the people. Prophets know that stable government is good for faith. And as long as things don't go too far Elijah is reasonably happy to run along in the rut created by Ahab's chariot wheel. The alliance between the ruling powers and religion has its point.

But things changed with the arrival of Jezebel, not so much because of her gods or her religion – that had happened before and accommodation had been possible. The problem was her crusading zeal to wipe out everything that had gone before.

It was also the effect this zeal had on Ahab. It had very little to do with the fact that Ahab and Jezebel were lining their own pockets. Rulers in all countries always had. The best of them provided land, sheep, cattle and vineyards, but people are not stupid, and they always knew that in a siege the castle would be the last place to collapse and the first to have the resources to recover. They also knew that even in peacetime it was always the case that what the king had given the king could also take away. All that could be taken for granted.

Nor was Ahab the first ruler to covet somebody else's plot of land like Naboth's vineyard. However, whereas Ahab and his like knew that either you couldn't have it at all or at least there were 'ways' of doing things, Jezebel had no such knowledge. Might was right. So the first confrontation is between Ahab and Jezebel.

But at the same time the effect on Elijah is not inconsiderable. Many of the things he and Ahab had always taken for granted were being destroyed. Life was being devalued – and always in the name of a better religion. The power of the state and the power of the institution seemed to be taking over and, combined, were knocking the stuffing out of Elijah and many of the people around him. Running along in the rut created by Ahab's chariot wheel was one thing. Living with the threat of a giant wheel grinding to dust everything that stood in its way was something else.

By this stage other images would be coming into people's minds. Ambulance workers, miners and seamen, health workers and educationalists, the Bar and the Temple, the City and the

CBI, countless members of Select Committees, back-benchers and Euro-MPs – sections of society all of which would have had little difficulty identifying with Elijah. But there is conflict there too. Right is not all on one side, surely! The listeners begin to feel the pressure of the conflicting forces in a new way, and wait with interest to see whether the end of the story has anything to offer to their condition that they had not thought or felt before. 'The Tale of the Chariot Wheel' has become a story of twentieth-century conflict in which the congregation are part of the drama. Yet at no point has the case been argued, have contemporary policies been criticized, current problems analysed, or sides taken. Indeed, today's world has scarcely been mentioned.

From this point the details of the story need no telling. One man against 450 prophets of Baal. Two bulls. Two altars. No fire. Taunt and tease the whole day. Finger nails nearly bitten off. Jezebel coming out at lunch-time with flask and sandwiches to learn the score. Then, a second altar, doused with water, is consumed with fire and Elijah slaughters the 450. No doubt now who was right. The day of the opinion poll had never been thought of, and this was not a day when anybody felt the need of one. They knew.

But you cannot end there, though preachers often have! Triumphalism is inadequate, as Elijah himself knew only too well, because it doesn't necessarily change anything, and what is the point of sending everybody home with the feeling that they were always right if everything else is as it was? For Elijah, the chariot wheel is still there! And he knows as he tucks up his robes and runs all the way to Jezreel[23] that the chariot is not far behind and is no respecter of persons. The wheel that has ground others into the dust – prophets, priests and bishops – will not stop at him. We need something more, and in the Elijah story there is not very much.

In the New Testament there is, because Jesus knew the same feeling. He too went along in the rut of the chariot wheel for thirty years, including pretty well half his public ministry. He saw what Elijah saw. He did what Elijah did. And the chariot wheel ground him also to the dust and left him an isolated figure on Calvary's hill – two arms outstretched to save! That is the moment to hear and reflect on Frances Young's poem on 'Institutions', which is about the crushing power of institutions and Establishment as they

> '. . . grind the dust and squeeze the juice of human tears
> To sap morale and break the back and bend the will,'

till in the end the prophet does get caught and crushed on the wheel. But as the wheel breaks up a cross is formed, the chariot catches fire,

> 'And the prophet rides the chariot higher and higher.'

For many listeners nothing more will be needed, and if this does not leave people facing judgment, pondering the issues, deciding with whom they wish in future to identify, it is doubtful whether such a deficiency will be overcome by any kind of overt appeal or exhortation.

Of birds and fishes

Beginning with the text, 'Two nations are in your womb, and two people, born of you, shall be divided; the one shall be stronger than the other, the elder shall serve the younger,'[24] think of Jacob and Esau as two nations.

The symbol of Jacob's people is a bird. Think of it, flying through the air. And the symbol of Esau's people is a fish. Think of that, swimming through the water. To begin with, the two peoples are not very far apart. One begins life in the water and the other begins life in the tree that overhangs the water. But it soon becomes apparent that they are totally different creatures. One is quick, with a desire to be on top and to 'go places'. The other is slow and content to swim around in circles. Go back far enough, and both came out of the same watery mass, but evolution took them in quite different directions. Neither is really responsible for what they are. They are what they were made. Some of us are birds and some of us are fishes.

How can we help the congregation to feel the closeness of Jacob and Esau in the womb, the totally different way in which they turned out, and the fact that neither could really be held responsible for being what they were?

At the same time as the Filipino peasants were reflecting on their own situation, Katharine Whitehorn[25] was reflecting on why it is that two children grow up together in a family and finish up so different. She attributed it to 'the parking lot' theory of human behaviour. When you go to a parking lot and see a car parked askew and looking awkward, you know that it was either put there by a very bad driver or (more likely) that it was put there because that was the only place left for it. And much the same, she suggested, is true of people.

So take a family of two boys. One is a holy terror and the other is Granny's good boy, quiet and respectful, always going out of his way to help. And everybody says, 'What a nice boy Jonathan is!' But do we ever stop to ask whether he is good because he is fundamentally different from his brother or because the role he has chosen is the only one left to him, the more interesting up-stage position already having been claimed by his elder brother?

Something similar may have happened to Jacob and Esau. Esau was first on the scene, a rough and ready man who loves hunting and doesn't care about his birthright. Jacob is a homely boy and the apple of his mother's eye. But maybe Jacob was compelled to be a homely boy because all the manly virtues had been claimed by Esau. And maybe Esau had to feign indifference to the birthright because he saw that Rebecca had made up her mind who was going to have it anyway. And so both boys, like so many of us, having sensed the roles they were meant for, went on to fulfil them.

From this point it should not be too difficult to cite instances from a selection of stories in the press or on television where two 'nations' are still fighting it out. These need not literally be nations. The subject may be a family, the community, the state or the world scene, but if the stories are told with emphasis on the feelings of the participants rather than the facts and the politics, or the rights and the wrongs, it should not be difficult for the congregation to latch on to one situation and make it their own, each in their own way. Once that happens, the story of Jacob and Esau, linked with the birds and the fishes, has helped us to appreciate a situation of conflict which matters to us in a new way.

We must now move on so as to understand the Jacob and Esau story better, and see if we can find light in our darkness. Try looking through the eyes of another culture: the Philippines, where the two nations are the nation of peasants and the nation of landowners. Peasants, sitting around in the evening contemplating their 'darkness', find themselves discussing land-ownership,[26] and one of them says,

> Where is it written that God gave the land only to Don José and the landlords? Nowhere! Where then did the landlords get the land they now own? From their parents' landlords, you'll say. And these, where did they get the land? From their landlord forbears, you'll say, who got it from their landlord ancestors. But I tell you, my friend, if we continue tracing the origin of landlord ownership, we must arrive at a time when our lands were grabbed by force from our own grandparents.

Then, in words that sound very like a New Testament parable, another peasant says,

> And how absurd is the argument of those who claim ownership over the land just because they were ahead of the rest in occupying it! They are like a person who went ahead to a theatre and claimed exclusive ownership over all the space – all the seats available – in complete disproportion to his or her needs. And when the rest of the people arrived, trying to get some seats, he forbade them – saying that because he had arrived earlier, he was now absolute owner of all the space.[27]

This fleshes out the two-nation theory and takes it one stage further. Things are not 'like this' just because 'that is how it is', but because somebody at some point made it that way and has a vested interest in keeping it that way. By now each member of the congregation may begin to wonder whether that is true of the two-nation hypothesis on to which they had latched. The Filipinos will help them take it further.

One peasant told his landlord, 'It's a bit as if you live in the world of the birds and we live in the world of the fish'. Birds move faster because they can fly. Fish move slowly. Some birds fly so high they never even notice the fish at all. (Jacob goes off and does his own thing.) Others want to be helpful and so urge the fish to imitate them – to fly this way and that way so as to move better. And the poor fish can't, because they live in a different world. So the best intentioned of the birds try again, and they offer a project here and a crash programme there. But the crash programme always crashes, and even the best birds become impatient and begin to shout at the fish because they are lazy and stupid, superstitious and resistant to change.

Yet the fish's-eye view looks so different from the bird's-eye view, which to the fish sometimes looks like the Tower of Babel – people trying to get as near to heaven as they can so as to be wiser than God. You can almost hear Esau from the world of the fish saying of his brother, 'Give him enough rope . . . One day he'll come a cropper.'

At this point we might be forgiven for thinking there is nothing we can do. Two nations it is. Two nations it will always be. Jacob and Rebecca obviously thought so, because they sent Jacob away from home. There wasn't room for both sons in the same house. Jacob should go back where he came from. Some situations seem irreconcilable, and birds and fish cannot share the same environment.

But then the Bible story says one or two clear things. Jacob and Esau must meet. Fear and anxiety on both sides must be overcome by the willingness to talk, to repent and to offer forgiveness. For that to happen, the initiative must be taken by Jacob. Jacob must come home. Birds must come down to fish, because fish cannot come up to birds, just as God had to come to earth in incarnation. And if some are feeling that this can never work because birds by nature eat fish and there is no way they can ever live together, what they are feeling is what fallen humanity has always felt. However, it has to be balanced by the picture of God's new creation in which the wolf can lie down with the lamb.[28] Of course in reality things may not work out just like that all at once, or even at all, but it is that hope and faith which has kept so many Jacobs and Esaus together.

If hope is our first problem, judgment is our second. We have to decide whose side we are on – whether we are birds or fish, and that depends which particular situation of conflict we latched on to in the first place. Still, either way it ought to be much clearer to us than it was when we started.

The power of darkness

In terms of story and narrative the New Testament offers rather less scope than the Old. Stories are altogether rather thin on the ground except for the stories Jesus told, most of which are parables with a stark simplicity in form which is their strength, but lacking in the shades of meaning and characterization that are more common in the older material.

Where stories do occur, however, there is often value in trying to open them up in a new way so as to bring out something that was not being noticed. Often this is due to one of two factors. Either people have very definite ideas as to what a story means, usually because that is what they were told in childhood or adolescence, or significant stories have acquired one meaning which effectively keeps out all others. So it happens that, preoccupied with the wood, we never see the trees.

By contrast, consider what John Taylor contributes to our understanding of the Day of Pentecost by putting it alongside an incident from Tolstoy's *The Power of Darkness*.[29]

> Nikita, the splendid, swaggering, wenching labourer, who settled down with his master's wife after she had poisoned her sickly husband, has now seduced her backward, sixteen-year-old step-daughter and murdered the baby at birth to conceal the fact from the girl's absent fiancé. During the wedding party he comes out into the cottage yard, thinking to make away with himself, and stumbles over the drunken form of old Mitrich, the odd-job man who once served in the Guards. Kneeling face to face in the stinking straw they weep on one another's shoulders. 'I love you,' cries the old soldier, 'but you're a fool! You think I'm a warrior? No, I'm not a warrior, I'm the very least of men, a poor lost orphan! Well, then, do you think I'm afraid of you? No fear, I'm afraid of no man! As I don't fear men, I'm easy.' To the cool spectator it is nothing more than the maudlin self-pity of two broken drunks. On the day of Pentecost also the cool spectators blamed the

drink. But to the guilty Nikita it was the hour of vision and new birth . . . A moment later, as Nikita begins his confession before the wedding guests, his old father cries out in ecstasy, 'God! God . . . it is here!'

It is the reference to Pentecost that gives the story its power, because it dares to relate a secular story of abject misery and darkness to one of the major festivals of the Christian faith and so *ipso facto* makes something happen in the heart and mind of the listener. There are questions. Am I hearing straight? Can you really relate these two events? What is the connection between the drunkenness on the Day of Pentecost and the drunkenness of these two labourers? Or was the Day of Pentecost perhaps a good deal darker than we ever imagine today because over the years we have been anaesthetized against the horrors of that experience? And there are not only questions, but anger in one listener and a glint of belief in the eye of another.

But then in case it should be missed, Taylor continues:

It is only a surmise, but I wonder whether something like that encounter did not happen on the Day of Pentecost. The elation of the resurrection appearances was over. They were without direction. There was nothing to do but wait. A reaction into fear, doubt or guilt would be likely. Did Peter then turn to John, Andrew to Philip, to share the despair that was in them? That would have been a deeper confrontation than they had allowed to one another before, the truth of the one exposed to the truth of the other, I and Thou. And so he was there – the Spirit – where the 'one' and 'one' was more than 'two'. The spirit of communion, the unity of the Spirit, possessed them in bonds of peace.[30]

Taylor's concern is to show how Pentecost 'happens' when one person is prepared to open up to another person. The preacher's task is to make it happen again. A useful bridge between Tolstoy's two drunks and contemporary Western society may be provided by recounting the incident when the bishop and the son of his spiritual director open up and confess to each other in Susan Howatch's *Absolute Truths*,[31] so that Pentecost today is not simply a recollection, a memorial festival, an application of what speaking with tongues may mean in our contemporary world or an explanation of the work of the Holy Spirit with a few stories to demonstrate how he is still at work today (though usually somewhere else rather than here!), but a present reality.

One way of doing this is to help the congregation then to call to mind people in their immediate circle who are sharing their despair, loss of direction, fear, guilt, and to encourage them to want to open up and see the results. They may be helped if they can come to see that once this happens and their friends begin to feel and respond differently there is nothing less than an expression of the Word of God in their experience. The Word of God is then no longer something hard and objective, like a tablet of stone or a Bible, but a reality, and when it has happened once and been recognized, it is more likely to happen and be recognized again.

Another way of overcoming traditional and hide-bound interpretations is to focus on one of the characters in a story who is normally ignored[32] or (following Taylor) to put the story down side by side with something else, similar or different. The problems of the two brothers, for example, may look very different if put side by side with the story of Cain and Abel or Jacob and Esau.[33]

A third way is to put a story in a different setting. The Good Samaritan in a contemporary setting in South Africa, Peru or Hampstead can come alive in a new way. But it may also help to focus on some aspect of the story which is often overlooked. The story, for example, tends to be used so much in terms of helping our neighbour that it is often overlooked that the question which gave rise to it was 'Who is my neighbour?' (not what should I be doing for him?), and the question which Jesus forced the enquirer to answer was 'To whom ought I to be neighbour?' From there it is not uncommon to suggest that we ought to show neighbourliness to the people we don't get on with, like the Samaritans. However, for the Scribes and Pharisees the sting was not in what Jesus was asking them to do or whom he was asking them to help; it was in the man whom he made the hero. Had the Samaritan gone by on the other side and the priest exercised a caring ministry, the story might never even have been remembered. The offence was the choice of hero and reject. Put that in a contemporary setting, making the hero the Muslim, a street person or a member of Sinn Fein and you have a story with a very different bite. Yet how many preachers are prepared to interpret this story so precisely in those terms today that members of their congregation scarcely want to shake their hands afterwards?

Something similar has happened to the Great Assize in Matthew 25, where Christianity is often interpreted in terms of putting our concern for the hungry and thirsty, the stranger and the naked, the sick and the prisoner before our pre-occupation with traditional religious duties. There is nothing wrong with that, provided that the thrust of the sermon is less an appeal to exchange a list of religious duties (burdensome or satisfying) for an alternative list of humanitarian duties, and more an appeal to lead people to feel where they have gone wrong and to sense new opportunities in which now they positively want to engage. But that is not the only thing the parable may be saying. Another powerful thrust of the story lies in the element of surprise which both parties feel when they suddenly see where they have been succeeding or failing, and (even more) when they suddenly realize the company they are in. A sermon which began with the title 'Surprise, Surprise!' and then went on to bring this out in such a way that self-confessed 'failures' began to be aware of their strength and self-appointed guardians began to be aware of their weakness, and both were led to sense the company they were in, would certainly bring joy to some and offence to others. But then presumably that was the point of the parable, and it would be particularly interesting to speculate whether the story was remembered and kept alive by those who were encouraged by it or by those who were offended. Either way, the sermon can only be said to succeed if by the end it has not only made people think but actually set up division, not necessarily within the congregation (though that cannot be ruled out) but within each member. More problems shaking hands in the church porch!

The matters of which I have been writing are not easy to achieve and may be much disputed. They are in any case simply examples and illustrations, and it is in questioning them, challenging their assumptions and disagreeing with them that other preachers may come up with other ways of achieving the same objectives. To make them work at all, however, it is already becoming clear that three things are necessary.

First, preachers have to do their homework. They have to have sufficient biblical skill to be able to choose and select their passages in the first place and to know what interpretations are, or are not, permissible. But then they also have to be ready to do sufficient work in the commentaries and the theologies to bridge the gap and to satisfy themselves that what they are saying will stand up under pressure and disagreement.

Secondly, they need a fair degree of imagination plus a lot of hard work to choose their phrases with sufficient care to make their impact. It is doubtful whether in today's climate preachers can do this as often as they are required to preach. Twice every week, bearing in mind all their other commitments, would certainly be excessive. Once a month, for this kind of utterance, might be more reasonable.

But thirdly, preachers need the capacity to handle the conflict they are likely to create as well as the pastoral heart to work with people who are troubled by things they have said and need help to work through their problems. If preachers can do this, provided that they see that what is happening is fair and worthy of consideration, their people will respect them even if they hate it at the time, as they come to appreciate that it is not the preachers who are getting at them. It might even be God.

2

Beginning with Life

From exploring the Bible in relation to life we turn now to interpreting life in the light of the Bible.

The key to 'preaching as theatre' is 'theatre' as a personal experience. It is the moment of arrest, of insight and perception. Like Moses with the burning bush or Lord Shaftesbury with the pauper's funeral it is the time when preachers 'see' what they have seen a thousand times before and never noticed. It comes to them in a new way and they find themselves taking off their shoes because suddenly they know that they are standing on holy ground. Such moments may be rare and fleeting, and for that reason they are all the more to be cherished. Their frequency and intensity may grow with practice, but how do we handle them?

First, by recognizing them, taking time to reflect on them and understanding why we must use them in our preaching. There are several reasons.

One, the incident that becomes alive for us is much more likely to become alive for the congregation.

Two, if the purpose of preaching is to make something happen, it is good to be able to demonstrate how things happen to us. It is not just food we sell. It is food we have tasted and learned to appreciate. We, too, get stopped in our tracks, are made to perceive and sometimes even forced to change direction. And if our job is to stimulate people to hear and see in a new way at the risk of having their whole life and attitudes changed, then they need to know that these same forces are at work on us, too. Grasping this and letting it be known that we have grasped it is but another way of bridging the gap between us and them.

Three, people like to hear sermons based on personal experiences. Provided the experiences are not too trite and preachers are not always talking about themselves, their families and their experiences or problems, and provided at the end of the day they get beyond their personal experience into something that has relevance and meaning for all, it helps others to identify with them.

Four, it enables preachers to bring out the awe in the ordinary in a way that requires little more than a sensitive eye. We can all be artists, sharing our vision with the congregation and perhaps helping them to appreciate it and to find their own way. Or maybe we can just make them more alert as they move around. What matters is not whether they share our vision (and certainly not whether they 'agree' with what we are saying!), but whether our vision helps them to see their own and whether what they see can stimulate them to action.

Kathleen Davey,[1] working with the Corrymeela Community in Northern Ireland in the early 1970s, was gardening one day in the front of Corrymeela House when the minibus deposited a group of young boys from one of the most violent areas of Belfast. Immediately they occupied a nearby 'chalet' and made it the base for a machine-gun attack on the big house, thus acting out something which was all too real in the streets where they lived. Kathleen continued working on her bed of marigolds and took no notice. After a while, when they tired of their activity, they came over to her. After a long pause one of the boys pointed to the marigolds and said, 'My God, them's lovely'. For a whole week they worked with her on the flowers, and at the end when they returned to Belfast she gave each of them a marigold. Three weeks later she got a letter. 'My marigold has died. Can I come back to Corrymeela?' Signed: 'With love. Your Little Gardener.'

But of course he couldn't. What he had to do was to transform his own world by growing his own marigold. We can none of us live on other people's visions and experiences, either past or present, nor even on our own visions of yesterday. Good preaching is not re-packaging other people's 'marigolds', and it is certainly not not telling people how to do it, but no more is it simply holding up a tapestry of ideals in the hope that they will catch something. It is enabling and stimulating them to find the vision for themselves.

Crucial to this is when we are able to go beyond the personal incident or encounter. Just as when we begin with the Bible it is important that we bring out the contemporary experience, so when we begin with the personal incident it is important that we allow the Bible to light up what is already there. If the beginning, for Moses, was puzzlement as to why the bush burned but was not consumed, the end was working through that experience until he heard the word of God in a new way, changed direction and saw similar change taking place in the life of those around him. It is this kind of encounter which we need to covet, explore and try to achieve for our hearers.

Because such experiences are personal, specific examples may be of less use here than in other places and call for more imagination and hard work to identify and unravel one's own encounters with the divine. However, in the hope that one person's experience may stimulate another's I give three examples of my own and one of how someone else's experience grabbed me and sent me off in a different direction.

The sound of silence

This was the result of attending my first Quaker Meeting and coming not only to a realization of the value of silence but also to the recognition of something which had been lacking in my non-conformist tradition. It set me off on a process of exploration which reached a point where I felt that others might benefit from sharing in the pilgrimage. Whilst it is in danger of becoming a sharing of ideas rather than experience, I tried to avoid the usual logical arguments in favour of a series of pictures. I also prepared them with an experience of silence and gave them an opportunity for an extended period of silence afterwards to enable them to 'feel about it' rather than to intellectualize it.

I began with Habakkuk 2. 20[2] and set the scene by simply recalling one morning when I was going about my usual business, how 'something happened' and how I responded.

A short while ago I attended my first Quaker meeting. It was during the Assembly of the British Council of Churches and we were meeting at the Friends Meeting House, so we worshipped in their tradition.

At first it was awkward, embarrassing! We sat there like stuffed sheep, some with eyes closed and head bowed, some with eyes open and a blank expression on their faces gazing into outward space, some craning their necks and gazing at the ceiling. It was 11.30 on Thursday morning. The next event was lunch at 1. And we sat.

After a full five minutes the silence was broken. At regular, if infrequent, intervals others followed. Nobody spoke for more than a minute or so. It wasn't a prayer meeting. It wasn't a debate. We weren't trying to relate to one another, to follow one another or to answer one another. Yet, in a strange way, the comments of each broke in on your silence, stimulated your mind and re-directed your feelings.

It was an experience of silence. I have often been told that silence is one of the neglected aspects of our Free Church worship. This experience set me off exploring silence in a new way.

From there I went on to share what I had discovered. My quest took me first, for example, to Meher Baba, an Indian sage through whom I learned something about the silence of God. Meher Baba lived a fairly normal life in and around Pune. He died in 1969 and for the last thirty-three years of his life maintained a total silence, though apparently he did communicate by writing. One of the reasons he gave for his silence was that all the talk and all the words of all the world's great religions had achieved so little. Nobody takes any notice. Why? Because God's communication is in silence, and if we don't respond to God's silence, what is the point of anybody adding words?

This alerted me to the silence of God I had been missing. The silence of God in beauty, in the lilies of the field. Yet we are all capable of stamping through a field of flowers without even noticing, and when we create our cities we create ugliness rather than beauty. The silence of God in order, with the migratory birds, with hibernation, with the rut of the deer in the autumn and the fall of the lambs in the spring. Yet we rarely pause to consider whether here God might be saying something crucial to us about the chaotic and disorderly way in which we live our lives, and when we meet our fellows we create chaos rather than order. The silence of God in the wonder of creation, when a tiny bird takes its first flight, a new-born duck its first swim, a calf stands up within a few minutes of being born or a baby begins to suck.[3]

I was beginning to see what I had been missing. My next step was more worrying. I began to realize not only how I ignored what God had been saying in the silence but how I had actually distorted it. This came as a result of reading some verses[4] in a book that came in the post and was quite unsolicited.

My blood knows where to go,
perspiration knows when to begin,
tears fall on cue.

If I were my blood
I'd take time off
every now and then,
take wrong turnings,
misinterpret instructions.

If I were perspiration
I'd arrive too soon,
hang around too long
and disappear when needed.

And if I were my tears
I'd forget to stock up,
I'd get low on salt
and leave without asking.

My body's in good shape.
It's upstanding and reliable.
We have so little in common.

I began to feel the wonder of God's creation and the failure of my attempts to handle it.

By this stage I needed to check my wanderings in the wilderness and got out my compass. Scripture. What about God's greatest moment of all – that moment of stillness, on a dark night, when

Jesus was born? That was God coming to earth in all his fullness. Yet there were no words or theories. That's what we introduced. We even called God 'the Word' and then had to build up all sorts of theories and add lots more words – Lord, Saviour, incarnation and atonement – in order to explain what really never need have been a problem in the first place. But God didn't do this. In most risky fashion God just put Jesus there in the silence of a dark night.

How I made the next jump I cannot remember, but I came to see that in the language of God silence and darkness (or at any rate semi-darkness) go together. I saw connections between walking through a leafy glade, with tall trees in the forest and sunlight falling intermittently across my path, and standing in the half-light of a Gothic cathedral, with its tall pillars and stained-glass windows; a connection which those who designed our cathedrals knew well and also knew how to exploit. I saw how skilled photographers can do all sorts of things with black and white, light and shade, half-light and silhouette, that they can never do with full colour or bright sunlight. I saw how silence in the world of noise is what half-light is in the world of darkness.

By this stage, sensing that some listeners might be lost in the imagery, I felt the need to say the same thing again in a different way, and a recent experience in Romania came to my aid.

I had preached in a Baptist church in Bucharest. It was a packed congregation, a huge choir, very wordy, very moving, very long. And the church significantly was ablaze with light. When it was all over one of the ministers said to me, 'You know the Orthodox Church has nothing like this. They never have any meetings for prayer and worship during the week.'

What he had forgotten was that that very morning he had left me for an hour in Cluj and suggested that I might like to sit in the cathedral. It was a cold, dark November day, and in that cathedral it was barely light. I sat by a pillar in silence. One by one I watched them come. The old lady doing her shopping. The middle-aged businessman with his brief case. The young woman with two children. The rough-looking fellow off the street. They entered in silence. They lit a candle to dispel the darkness. They knelt, they prayed and they left.

So I reminded him. I would certainly never have suggested that one was right and the other wrong, and I knew full well that I would never want to have to choose between them. But I felt in a new way that for the wholeness of God we needed both. For once I 'knew' what previously I had only been 'listening to'. Silence was no longer just the cessation of noise, like the stopping of a factory engine; it was something rich and positive that communicated.

But why, I began to ask, should such positive and creative silence be God's specially chosen form of communication? Could it be that whereas words and thoughts communicate with the mind, silence communicates with the feelings, and that since we can produce all the defences we need against thoughts and ideas but are much more vulnerable when it comes to feelings, it is much easier for God to get through to us with our feelings than it is with our minds?

This idea then took me almost to my last port of call, Ingmar Bergman's film *Winter Light*, which finishes in a cold church, on a wintry day, in semi-darkness as the sun sets and communicants gather for worship. One of them, a Christlike figure, though deformed and unattractive to look at, says to the minister,

> Think of Gethsemane, Pastor. For three years Christ had been talking to these disciples. And they hadn't understood a word he said. They abandoned him . . . the whole lot. But that wasn't the worst thing, even so! When Christ had been nailed upon the cross, and hung there in torment, he cried out, 'God, my God, why hast thou forsaken me?' He thought his Father in heaven had abandoned him. Surely that must have been the most momentous moment of all? I mean God's silence. Isn't that true, Vicar?

The minister answers numbly, 'Yes, yes'. And the film ends.

Now of all the people in the film, the minister seems to have been least touched by faith. Many Christian commentators have been disturbed by the end and have tried to find explanations for it, even to the point of suggesting alternatives. But it seemed to me that Bergman had deliberately left the minister hanging, and he suggested as much in an interview more recently when he said that what he was really saying was that even if God is silent, you still have to get on with what you are doing because God is still there, somewhere inside, and silence can communicate in a way that words never can. As Dean Inge once wrote, 'The silence of God has always been a great trial to mankind.'[5]

By now my quest was nearly complete, but perhaps I still needed something to earth it for others, especially those who found ideas difficult, and it had to be something that might touch their own experience. I thought of a broken marriage. When a partner in marriage is unfaithful and then returns to make it up, there is something much more important than the partner saying, 'It's all right, I understand. I forgive. Let's start again.' It's more of a silent look which says, 'I know . . . and it hurt . . . but let's forgive, forget and start again.' And if our silence can communicate that, is it really so difficult to appreciate the silence of God? Nor will the situation be helped if the defaulting partner keeps asking for reassurances. The couple will be much more helped by the silence of the partner which says, 'I know . . . and it still hurts . . . but I still understand', as they try to grow out of their experience together.

Perhaps this was not very different from what Meher Baba meant when he wrote, 'Let your minds sleep, so that your hearts may awaken to love'. The person who can say this, far from finding it difficult to be aware of God, is more likely to find that he or she cannot escape God.

If anything was going to happen among the hearers it had probably happened by now, only I could not leave it there. I needed something to reinforce the sheer power of silence. Kafka came to my aid.

In ancient Greece the Sirens were those mythical women who were so beautiful, so powerful and sang so sweetly on their island that they lured every ship within earshot on to the rocks, and the Greek hero, Odysseus, only got by when he had put wax into the ears of his crew so that they couldn't hear. Kafka has a comment on this story. He says that it is conceivable that someone might escape from the *song* of the Sirens, 'but from their silence, never'. Why? Because the silence is inside, and inside is the place where God speaks.

The drowned and the saved

This sermon took its rise in a night and a day when I was stranded in Paris. I was on my way back from Geneva, and Gatwick was fog-bound. This considerably sharpened my perception of how we all react in a crisis, forced me to look again at a familiar New Testament story, and afforded an opportunity to interpret the experience on four different levels.

Level One was simply a description of what happened – human beings in a crisis. I found it a fascinating study in human behaviour. Some people accept their fate without complaining and without emotion; they sit alone at table, as if all meaning has gone out of life and they no longer want human contact. Some rush madly from one phone to another, changing Swiss francs to French francs, phoning it seems not to matter whom. Some (of both sexes) use the situation as an occasion to flirt; air hostesses doff their uniforms and take to civvies, approachable now no longer as officials but as people. Some just eat and drink. Some just drink and eat. Some become offensive and aggressive. Nice, friendly people, no doubt, who normally have a light evening meal (which they had already had on the flight) and a hot drink before they go to bed, suddenly begin politely by asking for dinner and then become aggressive in their demand for food when they learn they can have it only if they pay for it. Some always have the latest rumour, others have the latest up-to-date information, and it soon becomes clear who will be the first for whatever it is that is going next.

Then I noticed how the mood changes. Once it is announced that there is a delay of an hour, faces drop. When it gets to two or three hours, there is a sort of panic: families have to be told, engagements cancelled. When you have lost a night and half the next day it doesn't seem to matter to anyone. Calm, almost leading to indifference, seems to have settled.

For want of better occupation, no doubt, I found myself wondering what would happen if we had to stay together for a week, or a month, or a year? Would we become like hostages? Or like the Jews in the concentration camps? And funnily enough, I was reading a book about Auschwitz at the time. Perhaps that's why I thought of it! Level Two therefore naturally became the bringing together of the two worlds.

Primo Levi was an Italian partisan, captured by the Nazis in 1943 and sent to Auschwitz, where he was one of the lucky ones who survived. *If This Is A Man* is a story of experience, and in one chapter, 'The Drowned and the Saved', he shows how the experience of living in camp seems to produce these two well-differentiated categories of men: the survivors and the capitulators.

Levi speculates why this might be. Perhaps it is because in the camp men are alone, in a way they are never alone in real life. Perhaps it is because in the camp the struggle for mere existence is at its greatest. But whatever the cause, Levi readily identifies those who quickly seem to lose all hope and strength and go straight to the bottom of the heap (the drowned), and those who have a unique capacity for staying alive (the saved). Then he quotes Matthew 25.29: 'to him that hath will be given . . . from him that hath not will be taken away'. In life, he says, this is a ferocious law. In the camp, it is recognized by all.

Level Three took me to the parable of the talents, and I recalled how once I got home I did some digging. The commentaries reminded me that 'talents' had nothing to do with 'gifts'. Jesus was talking about real money and resources, and whatever we had we were meant to use. I discovered also that Jesus was probably quoting an old Jewish proverb, simply saying that in real life it too often seems to be true that the rich get richer and the poor get poorer.

That put it very sharply. This story now was our story. It was the crisis we were all involved in, all the time. We needed to recognize it in our own country, and to keep it in perspective we needed to recognize it in other countries and cultures. I cited Britain, where since the end of the Second World War, in spite of twenty years of socialist rule, the gap between rich and poor had got wider, and where, in a year when we had all suffered from a doubling of VAT (1980), those on the highest rates of tax had been given a big enough tax deduction to do more than cover it.[6] I changed the scene by referring to families where, as Shakespeare put it, 'when troubles come they come not single spies'. We all knew families who seemed to have every misfortune and others to whom nothing ever seemed to happen at all. I opened the paper and read a piece about some Stone Age Indians in the Amazon whose numbers had been reduced from 4 million to 120,000 by the infiltration of the white man – they had been massacred by illegal settlers, bombarded from the air by hired gunmen, given food laced with arsenic and handed out clothes laced with disease. And all so that the settlers could exploit their land for a few years and then move on.

Primo Levi, in that situation and with that scriptural reference, had opened my eyes to at least three things I might otherwise have missed. None of it was new, and yet now, in a new way, I *knew* that what Jesus said was true. *They* knew what Jesus said was true. And *the hearer* knew that what Jesus said was true as well. To him who has will be given. And from him who has not something will be taken away.

Level Four was trying to work out what Jesus made of it. I used to think that he was simply saying that we all had something, and that if we used our resources well, a little trading here and a little daring there, then we would grow and do well. But if we tried to conserve our resources, we would finish up with nothing. Now Primo Levi and personal experience were forcing me to consider whether Jesus might be saying something different. I re-discovered T. W. Manson's paraphrase of this verse:[7]

> To him who has added something of his own to what I entrusted to him, more of mine shall be entrusted and he shall have abundance. But from him who has added nothing of his own to what I entrusted to him, shall be taken away what I entrusted to him.

This seemed to be exactly what Primo Levi was saying after Auschwitz:

> The Drowned seem to have nothing . . . the divine spark is dead within them . . . they are the non-men who march and labour in silence . . . through no fault of their own, they are overcome before they can adapt themselves, and they follow the slope all the way to the bottom, like streams that go down

to the sea. In Auschwitz the end is the gas chamber, and they
finish up there in their thousands.

But there are others, the saved. To begin with they are not very
different, but they fight to survive and they win. There is
something inside them – Levi says, 'call it five talents, if you like' –
and they come through almost with flying colours. As I looked
back at those families, and the Amazonian Indians, and the
people who seemed to have nothing, I suddenly began to identify
and recognize those who had that spark that enabled them to live.
Something was happening to me. Never again could I read that
parable without seeing it differently. And as I looked at the
casualties of life in all kinds of ways, I began to see them and
respond to them in a different way.

That left the hardest bit of all – taking away from the third man
even that little bit that he had and giving it to the others. I turned
back to Manson. What Jesus is saying, says Manson,[8] is that if we
fail God's work will still go on, only it will go on without us. And
our talent or opportunity will be given to someone else.

But did that then put a fresh complexion on the failures? On the
disciples, who failed because they were trying to save themselves,
and even on Jesus, who was crucified because he refused to
compromise? All were lost opportunities. One by one the lights
were going out, and the last one went out with the cry of
dereliction on the cross. But as the light went out on Golgotha
there was a glow in the garden. The future, after all, was not to be
with the saved but with the drowned, as God takes their lost
opportunities and gives them to others. Jesus dies, and the
disciples become new people. The disciples die, and the church is
born. The church suffers persecution, and the faith is strength-
ened. The story is a pointer to the resurrection.

God of the mountains

This turned out to be an invitation to share an experience in three
parts. It was a re-examination of my understanding of God at the
very point where I was most in love with him. At what point
would the listeners identify positively, at what point negatively,

and with what result? Any suggestion that my experience was to provide a solution or an answer or even a new view of God was to be avoided. My hope was that as I led my listeners along the road, they would feel the challenges for themselves and come to their own judgment.

Scene One told how, cruising in the Arctic Ocean, I became lost in admiration for the mountains of Norway and thrilled with the connection between their power and magnificence and the God I worshipped, until I saw that God on two legs and hated him. Scene Two described how I found an alternative, better but still unsatisfactory. Scene Three showed how through the experience I came to an understanding of God that I had not seen so clearly or so sharply before. I began with the rocks.

Walk along the shores of Cornwall or Pembrokeshire, the west coast of Scotland or the Outer Hebrides and you find rocks – huge lumps of granite going back thousands of years. I love them. They have always seemed to me to epitomize the God who was there in the beginning.

But not until I crossed the Arctic Circle in Norway and sailed the fjords of the far north did I realize you could have whole mountains of the stuff – hard, bare, black, and going thousands of feet straight out of the sea into the sky. If those rocks on our shores suggest God, then those mountains must surely be the place where he lives. Perhaps they are even God himself . . . always there, always the same, always beyond our grasp. And perhaps that was why Moses found him in Sinai.

The experience led me to catch up a bit on Norse mythology and I rediscovered Thor, the God who gave his name to Thursday. He lived, so they said, in the heavens above those mountains, and when he drove his chariot the mountains trembled and cracked; there was a mighty boom and the earth was scorched. What a God! He was around in the early morning, he was still around late at night . . . always busy, always running after time. He was powerful. He had a hammer for imposing his will; and he could make it as big or as little as he liked, but when he took aim he never missed.

I liked this God. He appealed to me. I felt his power. He could do the things I was unable to do, and we were living in a world and at a time when that sort of action was desperately needed, though I could not disguise the fact that the very language in which I had described him suggested to me, and doubtless to others, a human being, exercising a powerful influence over the British people at the time, who fitted that description to a 'T'.

But then when I looked more closely I found others who fitted the same description. They were people who had found this God and become like him. The Victorian grandfather: a strong upright (upright?) character who controlled the family's destinies (usually because he controlled the purse strings) and without whose say-so nothing could be done.

Men like Ephraim Tellright in Arnold Bennett's *Anna of the Five Towns*. He was a man of enormous wealth married to a woman of enormous wealth, and in the Potteries he had few rivals and fewer friends. Anna is his grown-up, unmarried daughter. She's twenty, and she's still frightened of him and his temper. On her twenty-first birthday she is as surprised as anyone when he calls her into the drawing room to tell her that she has inherited her mother's fortune. With Methodistic scrupulosity he then proceeds to hand it all over. Now *she* must take responsibility for it . . . it's her's! And she can't make a decision, because with 'a god' like that she's never been free. And anyway, he's got no intention of letting her, because it is the nature of this god to rule.

Anna loves him and hates him. 'Kissing,' she says, 'was not in the Tellright tradition' (well it wouldn't be, would it? The God of the Mountains is hardly a kissable god), 'but she had a fleeting wish to hug the tyrant'. She may indeed have wanted to hug him, just as something in me responds to those mountains, but I don't think she would ever like him. And the more I see of this God of the Mountains on two legs the less I like him, too.

He's so fixed and rigid – great on the Ten Commandments, but weak on people and their funny little ways. Thor, too, they say, is neither wise nor subtle. He plunges in blindly. He blunders and then gets stuck. And sometimes he gets so angry you can see the fire flashing in his eyes.

I felt the time had come to enquire if the description reminded them of anybody. I wanted them to feel the forces I was talking about. Is this the impenetrable force that too often leads to confrontation? Is it the blunder that leads to banana skins? Is it the power that makes the hammer so big and the aim so sure that in the end nobody can win but God? Is it the anger that threatens democratic rights? And the stupidity that could so easily start a nuclear war? I began to fear it might be, and sensed that if this is the God of the Mountains, then thank you, but I don't think I want him.

> Yet to think that to begin with I thought I liked him. Now my glorious God of those Arctic mountains begins to fade. I sit on the coastal steamer and I see his feet of clay . . . and clay spreading up to his knees and thighs, and like Mary on the resurrection morning I want to say, 'They have taken away my Lord and I don't know where they've put him.' Because if this is God, then it is God without Jesus.

As I nursed my wounds and disappointment, not to mention all the implications of my conclusion, I suddenly saw a new possibility and launched into Scene Two. I suddenly saw a waterfall out of the corner of my eye.

> Stupid things, waterfalls. You never get mountains without them. They all begin up there, with God in the mountains, and when they grow they get too big for themselves. There's no room to contain them, and they are so proud they think they can defy gravity . . . they go to the edge and step off . . . and they come crashing down into the bottom . . . absolutely oozing with power and energy, and all totally uncontrolled and undisciplined. All over the place!
>
> But this is where you find life. This is what makes the earth bring forth and blossom. And this is the God of the Mountains too, only now it is the God who is in turmoil rather than the one who is unchanging and intractable.

If you find the God of the Mountains in the Victorian grand-father, then you find the God of the Waterfalls in a bunch of noisy teenagers. A weekend colour supplement gave me potted stories

of five 'country kids' absolutely bursting with energy, ideals,
vigour and enthusiasm . . . all of it good . . . and yet, like a
waterfall, so much going to waste, and mis-directed . . . and some
of it possibly abused . . . their village (world ?) just not big
enough to hold them.

Or there was the girl who was given the freedom of the house
for her first party and was too lavish in her invitations. Her
mother shuddered as she saw the hordes rolling in. She spent the
evening next door in the granny flat and trembled. At four o'clock
she was awakened by the sound of breaking glass . . . the empties
being thrown out! Next morning she was told the house wasn't
ready. A tiny minority had got out of control. But then another
tiny minority had done all the cleaning up, and even some of those
who had done their worst were back within a few days to
apologize, do the repairs and the decorating.

These are the waterfalls – an uncontrollable excess of efferves-
cent life and the turmoil that goes with it – and it is in that
waterfall rather than the granite that we find the life of tomorrow,
whether we see it in the teeming life of adolescence or the teeming
life of Africa and Asia, or in some of the more revolutionary
movements of South America.

> This is the turmoil of life that goes with living, and Jesus is
> turmoil, and Jesus is life. The reason we often fail to think of
> Jesus as turmoil is that we've anaesthetized him. We've turned
> him into granite. But the Jews had no doubt that he was
> turmoil, threatening the God of the Granite Mountains whom
> they had worshipped for 2000 years. Herod and the Romans
> had no doubt that he was turmoil, threatening law and order,
> turning aside for the underdog, and challenging their tradi-
> tional values and way of life.

As Scene Two ends, I have identified a God of a different kind and
I have closely related him to Jesus. This God I like. He is much
better than the God of the Mountains. But somehow he is still not
right, and in Scene Three I have to work out why.

> My problem is that I can't live in turmoil all the time. I need
> something fixed to which I can return. Maybe Jesus did too.

Adoring crowds and palm branches were one thing. Rejection in the synagogues and Good Friday were another. That must explain why he had to climb the mountain, and perhaps if I could climb the mountain with him I might discover the life for myself.

And the thought of climbing the mountain with him took me back to the waterfall. Now I had to climb the mountain with a difference. Once I see where God is really at work I know I can only return to God through the turmoil of the raging waters. That is what took me to the salmon. It is the only way back. The salmon must return to the mountains to fulfil itself, but only by swimming upstream, against the current, and coping with the falls at the point where the current is strongest. And whereas to begin with I could only see God in the mountains, as through a glass darkly, now I began to see him face to face.

This, I thought, is a God worth having. Martin Luther knew him. 'Here I stand, I can do no other.' And when I find this God on two legs I like him even more – the politician with the courage to resist the whip, the trade unionist with the guts to cross the picket line, the whistle-blower and a thousand others who are prepared to fight the toughest corner, often in a minority of one, because something inside them requires it.

At that point I remember Ibsen's *Enemy of the People*. The hero is a doctor, utterly devoted to his patients and the local community and lauded to high heaven because of it until the day he incurs the wrath of the business and civic dignitaries by daring to suggest that what they are doing to the local water supply is injurious to people's health. All attempts to bring him into line fail, and as the play proceeds the tide turns. To begin with he is a man who stands for truth and righteousness. Everybody is with him, waving their palm branches. They have waited long for a man like this. Until suddenly they see the price they are going to have to pay. And at that point they hound him out of their self-constructed, petty-fogging synagogues. They follow him home and break his windows. His daughter comes home in the middle of the morning, having been sacked from her teaching post – the headmistress was very sympathetic, of course, but, well, there were the governors and she had no alternative. And his two small boys come home bruised and battered, sent home for the day because the other boys have gone for them in the playground.

The big question, for the man and his wife, is do they stay or do they quit? And after that dark night of Gethsemane they decide to stay, for even when the boot is in and the world is collapsing about his ears, he says he is the strongest man in the world. How? The last line is the best: 'Because', he says, 'the strongest man in the world is the man who can stand alone.'

> There is a salmon, I say, who knows he has to go back through the turmoil to where he belongs. There is a Christian who knows he has to swim against the toughest current. There is a man who knows he has to stand alone.
>
> And this is where I found the fullness of God in today's world. Not in the granite or the Ten Commandments. Not really in the waterfall or the excesses of youth. But where a person is prepared to fight the masses at the hardest point and win through. The end may be a cross. But it is in that cross that there is life.

Once again the language is intended to suggest other scenes and other places. References to trade unionists and whistle-blowers root us in the present, but references to palm branches and synagogues take us to other places and another person, and the listeners are left with a choice. They can keep it in their minds at the level of understanding. They can let it take over their lives and become different persons. They can do both or they can do neither. They can go off in other directions or they can stay exactly where they are, but if they are left in no doubt that whatever they do, this is a moment of judgment – something has happened.

'The Bag Lady'

Dan Hook, a teacher of homiletics in Australia, attributes the story of 'The Bag Lady'[9] to a minister in an inner city suburb of Sydney, where there are many poor people living and sleeping on the streets and in the parks, and uses it to illustrate his point that preaching involves much more than the communication of ideas. It is about experience of God and conversion, and the language of story may provide a new approach. It is a story that offers several possibilities.

First, it could be used as an illustration of a point which the preacher had already made in a sentence and wanted to drive home. It could illustrate the importance of hospitality, occasions when we entertain angels unawares, the Word of God coming from unlikely sources, the need for rebellion on the part of the young and change on the part of the old, and what happens when the resistance to change is too great. However, in every case the preacher would be imposing a 'meaning' on the story and 'telling' the congregation what to think.

Second, it could be told straight, the hearers being left to make of it what they will. It certainly doesn't need any introduction, explanation or moral precept. This is the method Dan Hook himself adopts, and then (since he is writing for preachers) analyses its construction. He shows how, to begin with, the hearer is an uninvolved observer of events with all kinds of other concerns and considerations. After a little while we suddenly realize that we are being drawn into it as involved participants. It becomes our story, and we find ourselves wrestling with the same issues as the characters. Something is happening.

Third, it could be told straight, but in a 'setting' which would encourage people to look at it a certain way. The setting may be simple, such as a word of introduction, a reading or a hymn, or it may be more direct if the story is set in the context of the Lord's Supper at a time when there is some conflict in the church or in society at large between the old and the new. Suitable readings before and after, highlighting the conflict between Jesus and the scribes and pharisees, would then add greater poignancy, but again it may be difficult to do this without loading the story a certain way and so depriving the hearers of their right to make a judgment and a choice.

Fourth, it could be told as a life experience through the eyes of the minister concerned, by a mixture of the straight story and his personal reflections on what it was saying to him, so enabling the congregation to share in the reflection while retaining an open-ended rather than a didactic approach. In this way the personal reflections become signposts for the benefit of those who have difficulty finding their way on their own whilst at the same time drawing attention to numerous highways and byways for those who want to wander, but certainly not telling them in detail what they ought to see or are going to find. What follows is the sermon on these lines which I might have preached if the story had happened to me.[10]

Hook tells us that the minister in question was used to callers asking for money or food, and though he was compassionate he was not one to be easily conned. One winter's night, however, the doorbell rang and on his doorstep was a bag lady, so-called because she could carry everything she possessed in a bag. He did not recognize her, but there was something about her, so he invited her in and offered her tea. She refused. She had not come to ask for anything. She had come to tell him a story.

'A long time ago,' the lady said, 'there was a village. It was not very different from any other village except that in the village square there was a table, and on the table was a loaf of bread. It had been there for as long as anyone could remember and nobody had ever touched it because there were dreadful stories around as to what would happen if anyone did. One said you would become a slave, another that you would be exiled and a third that you would die.

Parents would bring their children when they were towards sixteen, along with the village elders, and ask them in public if they wanted to take the village bread, and of course because of all the stories they had been told they always said No. So every daughter grew up like her mother and every son like his father.'

This may be the first point to pause and reflect, and at the same time to put up a signpost. What is this 'loaf of bread'? Is it the symbol of the various taboos and traditions that keep society in order? If it is, then it might be worth saying so and even identifying one or two. Not only will it help the listener to latch on to something, but it will also make the point that this village is no exception. Every village has its 'loaf of bread'.

Most villages, too, can tell the story of the day when someone touched the loaf. Martin Luther said, 'Here I stand, I can do no other'. If the church has got it wrong, then I have to say so. 'I will touch the bread.' Touching the bread is the action of a Gorbachev, who says, 'Communism Rules OK, but not the way we've been doing it'; or a Yeltsin, who says, 'Not even Communism at all'. It is the action of a Nelson Mandela, and perhaps even of a de Klerk; of a Salman Rushdie, a Martin Luther King, and even a Rosa Parks who refuses to give up her seat to a white person on a Montgomery, Alabama bus.

In another context over the same period the action may be that of a homosexual who 'comes out', a couple who decide to live together without getting married, a single woman who decides to have a baby but doesn't want a relationship with the father, a father who doesn't see why he can't have custody of his children when his wife leaves him, a doctor who administers a high dose of painkiller or a nurse who blows the whistle on him. There are 101 ways of touching the bread.

Feet having been kept on the ground, the story may continue.

And so it was in the village. One day, a lad, brought by his parents at sixteen, and asked by the elders if he wanted to take the bread, said, 'Yes.' The lightning flashed, the thunder crashed, the elders stood in amazement gazing at one another and his parents were shattered. If only they could have known before they produced him, it need never have happened!

But no sooner has the lightning abated, even a little, than normal service is restored. It was a blip. A flash in the pan. A one-off. The village, the church, the system – they all have their defences.

First defence. Does he know what he's doing? Has he been told? Because if he had, he couldn't possibly behave like this. Oh yes! he's been told all right.

Second defence. Then he can't understand or realize the consequences. Take him away and explain. So they do, and they ask him a second time, 'Do you want to take the bread?' 'Yes,' he says. More thunder, more lightning, more amazement, and parents even more shattered. 'Son, why hast thou

thus dealt with us?', as they said to Jesus when they found him
in the Temple at the age of twelve. Never have the elders met a
case like this before. But no society surrenders its taboos and
traditions easily.

Third defence. Try him a third time, and if he says 'Yes' this
time we really are in trouble. He says 'Yes' the third time. They
give him the bread and run for cover.

So, stand back! All hell will be let loose! And of course it's a
kind of self-fulfilling prophecy. Society hides in the bushes, or
below the parapet, and waits.

And sure enough, something happens. Only not quite what they
were expecting. Instead of disaster, what we find is the emergence
of love. Whether the lad had any understanding of what he was
doing is not clear – in a way he was a kind of sorcerer's
apprentice. He certainly knew that to touch bread was to take a
risk, but he decided that it was a risk worth taking.

If only they had known their New Testament better, they might
have known better what to expect. Jesus could easily have told
them. Had he not taken the same risk himself? At twelve, in the
temple, he was bold enough to chart out a course for himself, and
as he followed it through, heads shaking and tongues wagging, all
sorts of things began to happen. But not the horrors people
expected. Lepers were healed, the blind saw, the deaf heard, the
dumb spoke, and so on. Nobody had seen anything like it before.
It was all good and yet people hated it. Why? Touching bread.
You shouldn't do it.

Pope John could have told them. He took bread on the day he
walked across the room and suggested opening a window on the
world. Terrible risk! It's hard today to appreciate the full force of
what he did because he did it, but many Catholics, some with
pleasure and some with sadness, can testify to the force of change
over thirty years which that action initiated, whilst the scars of
Northern Ireland over the same period testify to the terror that
strikes in the heart of many when the world changes even a little.

Rosa Parks could have told them. She took bread when she
refused to give up her seat to a white person in that packed bus.
That was in Alabama. My first visit to Mississippi was in the long

hot summer of 1967. I spent a couple of days with a few whites who were helping blacks with voter registration. They were taking bread. They had to move their office from the main street to the back street because white Mississippians did not like to see black people in an office in the main street. The animosity these white reformers said they received was unbelievable. There were only about two restaurants in the town that would serve them. And they told me when I left not to say where I had been, or I would be ostracized for taking bread too. I thought they must be paranoid, until three days later in Tennessee I let it be known to some white Mississippians where I had been, and in an instant you could have cut the atmosphere with a knife. Watching the film *Mississippi Burning* could produce the same effect. Both demonstrate what happens when a few people take bread and love breaks out.

And still we have difficulty coming to terms with it, from Pakistani umpiring and damaged cricket balls through to unemployment figures and immigration controls. All fan embers that should have faded long ago.

Perhaps this explains a little why Jesus was cautious if not reluctant to invite people to walk this way. He had high hopes of Simon Peter, but even after the resurrection he was still checking and testing.[11] Simon, son of Jonas, do you really want to take bread? Yes, of course! It's usually thought that Jesus asked three times because he was unsure of Peter's love. Peter seems to take it that way and almost to be angered by it. But it could be that Jesus wants to make sure that nobody takes bread unless they really understand what they are doing. And if the elders in the story told by The Bag Lady kept asking because they didn't want anybody to break the spell, it could be that Jesus kept asking because he couldn't think of a reason why anyone would want to when they realized what had happened to him.

And so indeed it was with the boy in the story.

After the incident with the bread he went about doing good and helping people in all sorts of ways. A slave, but not servile. He went to neighbouring villages and did the same. A new spirit was born. And then one day he came back to his own village, where he found that the new spirit had taken over to such an extent that people were taking charge of their own lives and caring for one another in such a way that they no longer needed all the old rules and regulations, traditions and taboos, and (what's more!) they didn't even need the elders. And the elders took him outside the city and put him to death.

Then the bag lady said to the minister, 'But Father, what would life be like if nobody ever took the bread?' And with that she got up and went out of the door. When she had gone, the minister noticed she had left one of her bags behind. Inside was a loaf of bread. She had given him two gifts, the story and the bread.

By this stage the story is likely to have raised many points, and even more emotions, most of them calling for little if any comment. If it leads into a celebration where people are being asked to 'take . . . and eat', even more so. But it may not be inappropriate to let the symphony fade away on a few quiet chords instead of a crashing finale.

I don't know why we are afraid of love . . . why we resist it in the first place . . . why we crucify it in the second . . . but we do.[12] It seems almost as if we have to. Perhaps, for reasons best known to ourselves, we have taken too seriously that text which says that it is more blessed to give than to receive, and forgotten that in another sense it is more blessed to receive than to give, and receiving is what we are so bad at.

But I do know that Jesus took bread and invited us to take bread too. And I also know that the bag lady was right. What would life be like if nobody ever did?

3

Beginning with Literature

Literature in this context may mean anything from the short story to the full-length novel, from the one-act sketch to the full-length drama, from classical to contemporary, written or electronic, stage or film. It is wherever life is presented in a creative or imaginative way. All is grist to the mill as far as the preacher is concerned and for many reasons.

First, preacher and writer share a common heritage, not to promote or 'preach' (despite the confusing terminology) but to hold a mirror up to life in such a way as to enable people to see themselves and to get a different view of the world around them. To attempt more, for the writer, would be to prostitute an art. To attempt more, for a preacher, would be to prostitute a calling and shade off into proselytization or indoctrination.

Second, preacher and writer are handling the same raw material – life and people. It is true of the Bible: long before it became sacred text or holy scripture it was stories of people reflecting their lives, their hopes and fears, joys and sorrows, successes and failures, struggles and disappointments. It is true of soap opera; the stories pass, the arguments fade, the quarrels come and go, but the people carry it forward.

Third, preacher and writer are aiming at the same part of the anatomy – not the head, though all good literature will have an intellectual quality about it; nor the will, though much literature may well change the way a person behaves; but the heart. As entertainment, literature may do little more than make people feel better; at other levels it may open up a whole range of emotions and stir their minds on all kinds of issues, but in the end of the day what happens will depend far more on the reader than on the writer.

Fourth, literature is a rich source of ideas and material. Provided preachers allow literature to speak for itself and do not misuse it by clipping all the little bits they want so as to use them simply to illustrate or boost the points they want to make, literature is full of seams waiting to be mined and sources rich for the picking, and (at its best) is focussed directly on the fundamental themes of life with which the preacher is for ever engaged: birth, suffering, life and death, relationships and judgment, forgiveness and reconciliation.

Fifth, once you grasp the overall idea rather than the detail, the predominant concerns of literature are so close to the literature of the Bible (particularly the Old Testament) that the placing of the two side by side will invariably enrich both. Good literature can give a feeling of immediacy and relevance which many readers find difficult with scripture, whereas the Bible can clarify overall direction and relate to a fundamental understanding of God who spans time in a way that the wide variety of literature confronting us often cannot. Moreover, experience suggests that not only does the one enrich the other, but together they make a new creation in which the voice of God may be heard more clearly.

Sixth, and most important, once preachers cultivate the habit of relating to life through scripture and literature, they will soon find that members of the congregation begin to do this for themselves. It is in fact the beginnings of genuine D-I-Y, and the preacher teaches not by telling people what they ought to know, believe or think but simply by practising certain lines of interpretation which with a little experience and guidance the listeners are quite capable of pursuing for themselves. So the old adage 'we never knew what sin was until we got our present minister' may give place to 'we now read a lot and watch a lot which a little while ago we would either have missed, dismissed or just switched off'. In this way listeners can become their own preacher-prophet-interpreter, though they will always benefit from sharing their experiences with others. If this could then be linked with a midweek Bible Study Group which learned how to move from the Bible to literature, or a mid-week Theatre Group which began by reading or watching plays and learned how to move from literature to the Bible, the preacher has already got the beginnings of a worship workshop which could enrich much that happens in the sanctuary even further.

Short stories are one of the simplest yet most effective forms of communication, drama one of the most sophisticated – one is the 'catchy tune, the other the symphony'. We begin with a short story by Kafka.[1]

'The Metamorphosis'

The heart of this story is the person who feels like 'a nobody', and the purpose of the sermon will be either to appeal to those who feel like that or to help those who don't to enter into the feelings of those who do. Though beginning with the former, we may nevertheless find ourselves moving more and more towards the latter.

Stage One uses the Kafka story to enter into the experience. 'Do you know how you can cause most hurt to someone with least effort on your part?' said the speaker on the radio. Answer: 'By treating them as if they were not there.' Imagine then a situation where you wake up one morning and discover that your son or daughter, brother or sister, has been changed overnight into an insect. He always locks his bedroom door so you can't get in. And now, because he is only a centimetre long, with six long legs, bulging eyes, and antennae stretching out to feel (where before he depended much more on what he could see), he just isn't in any position to get up out of bed and let you in. Neither can he get up and go to work. What would you do? The idea is that of the Czech writer, Kafka. The name of the insect is Gregory.

Stage Two then earths the Kafka story by talking about real people so as to bring out the human situation and put it alongside a parallel Bible passage.

Many Africans, for example, feel like this all the time, and the media regularly report instances of blacks in this country for whom it is not an infrequent experience. All one has to do is either to focus on an instance recently in the news or an isolated case which will readily be regarded as typical. There was the little black girl, for example, who dearly wanted to be an angel in the school nativity play but knew she hadn't a chance. All angels in

her school were white and blonde! Or the black boy who said that
if he drank from a bottle and passed it to a white boy the white
boy would hold it some distance from his lips and pour it into his
mouth, though the black boy couldn't help but notice that he
never did that when he got it from a white boy. And not only the
blacks. The unemployed, the people on various forms of benefit,
the mentally ill and people with various forms of disability feel it
all the time.

Once launched, the idea can be taken further and in different
directions. Some of the poorer nations feel it when they have to go
begging to the rich. People who run small businesses often feel
it when competing with their more successful competitors.
Churches feel it. And then, to return to the personal sphere, is
there anyone who cannot recall what it feels like to go into a room
and feel totally ignored or to be by-passed completely by their
closest family at a time when they desperately needed help?

In other words, what at first seemed somewhat outlandish
turns out now to be one of the commonest experiences of life:
feeling just like an insect when yesterday you were a person. Some
feel it all the time. All feel it some of the time. The important thing
is to get people to feel it and give them the option of identifying
with it themselves or of feeling it in relation to others.

The next step depends on how you, as preacher, read the Kafka
story. What struck me was Gregory's ability to cope with the
problem despite the odds, particularly if he got help. The real
problem was not so much the fact that he was an insect as the fact
that other people couldn't cope with him as an insect, in this case
his own family. That was what made life impossible, not least
because they were totally unable to relate to him and lost contact
with him to the point where he was made acutely aware that in
addition to all his difficulties his terrible condition was so
distressing to them. He would have had little difficulty identifying
with the psalmist who said, 'I am a worm and no man; scorned by
men and despised by the people.'[2]

Again, raw material from life is not at all difficult to come by.
When people are hurt or rejected or passed over for promotion, it
is often the case that their problem is intensified because, though
they may be able to come to terms with their humiliation, their

spouse, partner or family cannot. A severely disabled person can often summon up the resources to live with limitations more easily than the healthy who have to sit opposite at table. Even Job found it more difficult to handle his problem once his friends came to 'comfort' him.

Stage Three is beginning to identify the strands in this desperate situation that require attention. We are all looking for hope, and in Gregory's case hope comes in the form of his sister. Clearly she doesn't like what she finds any more than anybody else. After all, what sister wants an insect for a brother? But at least she manages to say, 'Still, he is my brother, and therefore I must care for him'. She is saying in her personal situation what Mother Teresa has been saying in Calcutta. Unpleasant smells and running sores are no less abhorrent to a nun than to the rest of us. Crime, injustice and exploitation are no less offensive if you live in the midst of it than if you live at a distance. And if we in a position of relative comfort are angered by emaciated bodies, how much more angry might you expect her to be as she moves in the middle of it all. 'Still, this is my brother.'

By now it is not difficult to introduce the New Testament for further light. The Good Samaritan[3] is an obvious story, provided we see it not as an injunction to treat people better but as a way of appreciating what it must feel like when you have been injured on the road of life and suddenly, after all the others have passed by, somebody actually stops. Then we discover that the person who stops is the last sort of person we would have expected. Anyone who has stood at the roadside with a flat tyre can enter into that one.

But it is difficult to have hope without judgment. Whether I am the victim or the onlooker, the story of the Good Samaritan compels me to ask other questions. 'For whom do I stop? To whom am I sister – or neighbour?' And although Gregory's sister spells hope, what becomes increasingly clear is that not even she is capable of coping with the situation, whilst his mother and father become even more detached, almost to the point where they would like to believe that he wasn't really there. Every day Gregory stretches out his arms (or antennae), desperately in need of a relationship, yet the closer he approaches with his arms outstretched, the more horrified and afraid people become.

Is this, then, really the way we feel about members of our society in similar circumstances? If the parallels have been placed side by side, without comment, 'oughts' or 'shoulds', it would be difficult for even the most insensitive member of the congregation not to feel something stirring somewhere. So why the fear? Are we afraid because we don't know what to do, or how to do it? Are we anxious because there seems to be nobody else around and, our weakness being exposed, we are having to admit our own need of someone? Or are we actually experiencing a moment of judgment because of our response?

Stage Four is the tightening of the net. As the listener, I am slowly being caught in a trap. On the one hand I am being forced to face some hard questions about myself. Why have I never seen this before? Why am I anxious, worried or hostile when the preacher forces me to look at it? What am I doing to change even my corner of society or family life so that people don't feel like this? But then, on the other hand, if I turn away from these questions I am left with the more difficult question why I feel the need to turn elsewhere. 'Whither shall I go from thy presence, whither shall I flee from thy spirit?'

Sadly, what Gregory's parents desperately wish is that, somehow or other, he would go away, and in the end even his devoted sister finds herself being forced to the same conclusion. This is an understandable emotion with which most of us could identify. They may find it hard to admit, but most parents who have cared for a severely disabled child over many years must have had moments when they felt just like that. Many more have felt it about the Gregorys of society, and there is something sad about the way the family are so relieved when in the end Gregory dies, killed by lack of attention, and they move house and life gets back to normal.

But the object is not to condemn them ('what a pity they couldn't cope!') nor even to feel sympathy for them ('well, you can understand it, can't you?'). It is to help the listeners to face their own hostility to 'Gregory' so that instead of hoping he will go away (and feeling guilty when he does), they can turn their awareness of judgment into something positive. This would be at least a change of attitude, if not immediately a change of behaviour.

The Tears of Lady Meng

If 'The Metamorphosis' raises questions about how we react to people who feel they are regarded much as the scum of the earth, then *The Tears of Lady Meng*[4] raises questions about the sort of society we want to create and the price we are prepared to pay for it. Is it one in which we are prepared to sacrifice other people to achieve what we want, or one in which we learn to share in the sacrifices of others? The sermon moves freely on three levels – Bible, legend and life – and we experience the shocks and concerns right up to the point where the cross is obvious to all. Again the questions arise in the story and therefore indirectly rather than directly; they are not academic questions to be answered or matters of the will about which something must immediately be done. But they do touch the emotions and therefore the place where something is likely to happen.

First, a biblical setting:

4000 years ago the children of Israel were building cities for the Egyptian Pharaoh. First they built Pithom. Then they built Raamses.[5] Whether Pharaoh wanted Pithom and Raamses is not clear. What is clear is that he wanted a confrontation with the children of Israel. Pithom and Raamses were just one way of building up the aggravation, and when that failed, as we all know, he resorted to much nastier tactics.[6]

Next, the Chinese parallel:

2000 years ago the Emperor of China was building a wall against the Mongolian invaders from the north. It is still there, more or less, 1500 miles long, some of the stones as big as granite, 14 feet long and 3 or 4 inches thick. Today it stands as one of the great marvels of China, if not of the world, but it was built at an enormous price. A million people, it is said, perished in its construction. Every stone a human life, like every

Flanders poppy petal at the Albert Hall Service of Remembrance.

Then, from yesterday to today:

> Both the Pharaoh and the Emperor were builders, and in order to build they had to crucify. Today, you and I are builders – we are all of us builders of a society – so do we crucify others in our building? Do we rejoice in confrontation – 'I reckon we've got them this time, they'll just have to give in'? Do we destroy the lives of others in order to build for our own protection – 'I know it's tough on those who can't manage, but it's either them or me'? What sort of wall do we build and at what price?

By now the mind should be ticking at three levels: the biblical, where we like to think we know what the right thing is; the legendary, where we want to know what happens; and the personal and contemporary, where we hope we will discover some wisdom. We will proceed on the personal and contemporary level at a time when many people feel as if they are being persecuted for not very much in return, either for themselves or for others.

> Consider for a moment some of the bricks which our leaders have led us to believe are essential to the growth of our society – high interest rates must come down, inflation must be reduced, production must increase, and so on. But at what price does all this building go on? And who dares to stop to see the high price being paid and who is paying it?

One or two specific examples could readily be cited, not in such a way as to focus on the unemployed, the disabled, the elderly or the like, but simply as a story of the price someone was asked to pay in today's world. The most recent examples from the press are the best, but the following may help to convey the idea.

Angela was successful in getting a job when she left school, thanks to a Mrs Blimp type of agency, where she lived in as a mother's help, doing housework and minding children, and all for £25 a week. 'Mrs Blimp' of Hampstead thought girls like Angela were spineless and needed that kind of discipline. 'Sadly,' she said, 'these girls live in a society where they are paid such benefits that they don't want to work.' Angela's mother saw it differently. She didn't think Angela was spineless. She just thought she was unlucky enough to be born in the early 1960s in a part of the country where jobs were at a premium. But then nobody cared much what Angela's mum thought, because she and Mrs Blimp live 400 miles apart and Angela's mum had never seen the inside of a golf club.

The other interesting character in the story is the woman Angela works for. If Angela's mum had gone to work she would have been told that she was neglecting the children, but for this woman it was different. She had a profession. She was single, in her mid-thirties, with two children under five, and, with a part-time lecturing job and Angela living in, she managed to escape most of the traditional female activity at the expense of one of her younger 'sisters' who had no choice but to take it on.

By now a number of ideas are running around and each in a way indicates the price being paid by different people to build a society.

Next, it is important to kill the idea that the people driving the engine are nasty people. Probably not. Many people who know Mrs Blimp personally no doubt like her, respect her and think she's doing a splendid job. People close to the Pharaoh and the Emperor probably felt much the same, because for every hundred who died there were a few more hundred doing very well. No doubt their children loved them and were thrilled with the toys they brought home. But then into this situation we have to drop the story of Lady Meng, who features in one of the many legends associated with the building of the Wall.

The story goes that every time they tried to build the wall it kept falling down – it was always going to work next year but it never did – so a wise man suggested that with a wall of that length you needed to immure a human being in every mile. They did this, and the slaughter was unimaginable, until a wise scholar suggested that since the name Wan in Chinese means 10,000, all they had to do was to find a man called Wan and it would be expedient that he should die for the rest. So they found him, at his wedding breakfast, seated beside his bride,

Lady Meng, and the soldiers came and carried him off, leaving his bride in tears.

In her despair she decided to search the walls until she found his bones, but since all her searching got her nowhere, she decided just to sit down. She sat and she wept. She wept for herself. She wept for Wan. She wept for all 10,000. And it was her tears that washed away the wall to reveal her husband's bones.

All of which seems to suggest that we shall only build a worthwhile society (wall) when we too are prepared to weep with those who weep and to share the sufferings of those who suffer, rather than to back the Pharaoh with his cities and the slaughter of the innocents, or the Emperor with his wall and the crucifixion of the victims. Because in the end what saved the children of Israel was the tears of the Pharaoh.[7] It was *his* tears that washed away the injustice when *his* firstborn died and he experienced first-hand what others had been going through.

Yet we all have difficulty in shedding tears – not crying, as if out of self-pity (though even that may have its place), but actually identifying with the sufferings of others to the point where it hurts. The temptation to back off is always too much for most of us. And so it was with the Emperor. Once Lady Meng's tears became painful to him, and once he saw his wall being washed away by them, he decided the time had come for action. He would make amends by an offer of marriage which she could not refuse. But he misjudged her. She knew that there was something else beside tears, and that was justice.

So she agreed to marry him on three conditions. One, a festival for forty-nine days in honour of her husband. Two, the Emperor must attend her husband's funeral. Three, a platform forty-nine feet high on the bank of the river so that she could make a sacrifice. He agreed. But then when Lady Meng ascended the platform she launched into a fiery speech denouncing him for all his wickedness. At first, he held his tongue. But then when she jumped headlong into the river he flew into a rage and ordered his soldiers to cut her up into little pieces and grind her bones to powder. However, all the little pieces changed into little silver fish, in which the Chinese say the soul of the faithful Meng will live for ever.

Some worshippers will get the point quicker than others, depending on whom they have been identifying with throughout the story. Those who have been identifying with the Pharaoh or the Emperor are clearly in for a shock when they see how things turn out. Those identifying with the people immured in the wall will find it easier. Those who have learned to weep with the tears of Lady Meng will find it easiest of all.

From there it is but a short step to the Cross – to the one who shared the sufferings of the outcast, the leper, the demoniac, the sick, the blind and the lame – and to the link between the tears of Lady Meng and the tears of Jesus over Jerusalem. And would not Herod and Caiaphas gladly have bought him out and taken him over, just as the Emperor wanted to institutionalize Lady Meng, if Jesus (like her) had not realized that his tears were only the first step on a new road to justice? Because he refused, they killed him as they killed her. They cut him in pieces, robe and all, as they cut her in pieces, yet today he too stands for ever as 'the life that will never, never die'.

But then, as the heart begins to weep, the conscience begins to stir and the will begins to act, the congregation needs someone in real life where they can see it happening. The preacher needs to have an example ready. Someone, some story recently in the news or on television, which has dispelled lethargy with the recognition of one in whom the tears of Lady Meng are still flowing. Through that person the congregation may begin to see. Better still, as the days pass by they may begin to find Lady Meng for themselves nearer than they thought. And here and there a few may actually don her mantle.

Waiting for Godot

Described by one critic as a play in two acts in which nothing happens twice, *Waiting for Godot* caused a number of problems to many people when it was first put on in the 1960s. Two questions arose. Who was Godot? And what did it all mean?

In February 1968 the Connaught Theatre in Worthing staged it for two weeks. I decided to see it the first week, preach on it the following Sunday and encourage people to see it the second week and to judge for themselves. Prior to seeing it I did almost no homework so as to allow it to speak directly. Whatever I said had to be related very closely to scripture. People were not used to sermons that made too much of the theatre, and since this was a point in my ministry where I was under suspicion for not being orthodox, my use of scripture was the ultimate test. In a moment of insight over a cup of coffee in the interval I decided my title was going to be 'Life is Three People'.[8]

The first thing was to establish relevance. Few worshippers that morning would even have been aware of what was on at the local theatre, and had even less awareness of Beckett or Godot. If they had, some would not have wanted any reference to it in the morning service, and others would have found it well nigh impossible to see much connection with the gospel. What all would find it difficult to object to, however, was a sermon on life, especially if it had some New Testament basis. So, having given them the title but (on this occasion) no text, I began:

> You can find the whole of life in my three people, and you can find my three people anywhere. They are here in the congregation, and as you go home you pass them in the street. They are everywhere in the Bible, and you have heard sermons about them Sunday after Sunday for years. This morning, by way of a change, I find them in a play by Samuel Beckett. Controversial it may be, but it is Christian drama at its best.
>
> My first person is the man who idly stands and waits. When he was at school he was waiting to start work. When he started work he was waiting to meet a girl. With many others of their kind they waited to get married, and then they waited on a long list for accommodation or a mortgage. They waited two years for a baby and then they waited nine months for it to arrive. He waited for promotion and she waited for the freedom that would come when the children grew up. They waited for retirement and the pension – until eventually they waited to die.

By this point the scene had been set and the everyday relevance of what we were talking about established; so too had the hearers' potential to determine the level and interpret what was coming.

The ball was in their court. But they were still not a little puzzled. It was time to develop the story. So I explained that in order to bring out the problems of the waiting man, Beckett invites us to think of him as two tramps waiting for someone to come. But the two tramps may be understood as one person, representing two sides of our human nature. The one is essentially a doer and a practical man, moved much more by his heart than by his head. The other purports to be a thinker, though he never has any remarkable thoughts. Each is something of an irritation to the other and yet each is indispensable to the other.

The introduction was brief but it serves a dual purpose. First, it establishes the point that my theme is not really about waiting but about people, some of whom I identify and some of whom I leave the congregation to identify, leading to questions which will challenge or sharpen these identifications. Second, it helps to build a bridge to the New Testament, because you can find these people there in the crowds that throng the highway. They are there when somebody is healed or when a story is being told. They are there when the scribes and Pharisees stage a fight. They are there on Palm Sunday, shouting Hosannas. They are there on Good Friday, shouting 'Crucify him'. Life for this character is never very deep, never very meaningful. One half feels there ought to be some meaning, but never quite finds it. It never comes. The other half just goes on waiting.

Time to move on.

My second person is the man who crosses the stage of history for the attention of the waiting multitudes. Sometimes he receives their admiration; often he provides diversion, entertainment and amusement. Life is not complete with the gullible masses. It also needs people with some kind of meaning to life and some kind of principle by which they live.

In Beckett's play this man is called Pozzo. The word means fool and he is a fool, but he is a kind of impressive fool who makes the tramps wonder. Pozzo is a man who has the gift of making the most ordinary things sound important and tremendous. Even sitting on a chair becomes a major operation for him. Going back on something he has said or done

previously is almost impossible, unless he can be sure he is
doing it without losing face. But in all his confusion he has
found one thing in life that matters. In his case it is time – his
life is built round a half-hunter. And when later in the play he
loses his half-hunter, the one thing he cannot bear anybody to
do is to refer to it.

It was possible to identify Pozzo in a number of ways and in each
case to cite some well-known personality who happened to be
dominating the media or the political, church or world scene at
the time. At one level he is the person through whom you think
you can escape from the monotony of living. At another level he is
the person through whom you think you can find some fresh key
for living. In church circles he may be the current evangelist or the
latest bishop to be involved in controversy, depending on your
theological propensities. In your family he is the one member who
thinks he or she can tell the rest how they should live, and in your
office he is the one person who likes to think he or she is a cut
about the rest. The net needs to be cast wide enough for listeners
to be able to latch on to someone and specific enough for them to
think of real people, but it is most important that the choice is
theirs and not the preacher's. (Again, this calls for one or two
judicious stories rather than a straight list as here.)

For me, however, the crucial person was the third one, though
he could not exist, nor could he have meaning and relevance,
apart from the first two. What I did not want to do was to 'sell'
him, certainly not to 'package' him, so it was a question of fairly
objective description which would leave the congregation with
options, but with little doubt as to where they knew they ought to
look and what they knew they ought to see. After that, it was up
to them.

My third person is the most impressive of all, whether you meet
him in Beckett, in the Bible or in life. The difficulty is that I am
not sure where you do find him. Let me describe him first as he
is in the play, and then see what you make of him.

His name is Lucky. Clearly he is a slave, and he is the slave of
Pozzo. He comes on to the stage wearing a great rope round his
neck, and leading Pozzo. He carries Pozzo's bags, and he obeys

Pozzo's commands. He has no life or character of his own, and he is not very pleasant to look at. He is supposed to think if you put his hat on, but the one and only speech that he utters is a load of codswallup. He used to dance for Pozzo's amusement, but he can now dance no longer. He is so weak and ill that he virtually dies on the stage, by a tree, in the shape of a cross. In life he is what people have made him; in death he is what people have done to him.

Following Beckett's use of symbolism, I chose language carefully to leave the congregation in no doubt as to where Lucky might be directing us, and in case they missed it I spelt it out. I quoted Isaiah 53: 'He had no form or comeliness that we should look at him . . . he was despised and rejected by men . . . like a lamb that is led to the slaughter, and as a sheep before the shearers is dumb, so he opened not his mouth.' The words were familiar enough, but not usually as a description of Beckett's Pozzo, so that by this time the listeners were beginning to work out whether we were in Beckett or in the Old Testament, in their own life or in the New Testament. A new problem was also emerging. Were Jesus and the Suffering Servant of Isaiah 53 going to help us to appreciate Lucky, or was Lucky going to give us fresh insight into the crucifixion? The uncertainty was enough to provide a situation in which something might happen. But it was time to sharpen things a little more. Another question.

Where do we find this person in life? Do we find him in somebody who is content – really content – to be used by others? Do we find him in the person who is prepared to lie down and take the kicks of life? Do we find him in the person who is prepared to carry the can for another, and to become just what that other person wants to make him? See this play, I said, and see if you can find through this third person what you have never been able to find through the biblical picture of Christ, because few people can have appeared on a stage bearing a closer resemblance to him.

In some congregations that would be the place to stop. The listeners can then write the final scene for themselves – may indeed have written it already! In other cases, particularly where listeners are unused to such treatment, it may be worth going on stage further and asking what this play says to us about life that is three people. This provides alternative finales.

The New Testament certainly doesn't say much to us about the crowds – they just wait. Nor does it have much time for the seven-day wonders – Jesus clearly had a horror of being one and rejected it firmly at the time of the temptations. But the whole emphasis of the New Testament does fall on this third person, and seems to say that when he is around, hopeless and helpless as he is, things happen and that lives are changed.

The odd thing about Beckett's play is that so far as I could see nobody's life was changed. I looked hard, and I would have liked to find it. It would have made my job so much easier. I could have pointed and said, 'Look what he did; look at the effect it had; go and do the same.' And I would have felt better if I could have seen some results from this man's sufferings.

But what Beckett taught me about Christianity – and I certainly hadn't seen it so clearly before – is that the real results are the ones that you don't see. Not in this life. This side of the grave we are all of us waiting for Godot. It is faith, not sight, that leads us to believe that the secret lies with the Luckys and the Christs, and that is why we have to tremble before them.

Or perhaps it isn't three people after all. Perhaps it is just three aspects of every one of us. The waiting tramps, Pozzo and Lucky are inside all of us, and Beckett and the New Testament together are trying to tell us which bit of our character matters most to God.

The Seagull

The Seagull came alive for me when I saw it as a play about ideals, and especially about Nina, who only discovers what her true ideals are when she is prepared to allow the ones she has to be blown sky-high and to endure all the pain and suffering that go with that. Once there, I saw it was also about other people with disappointed ideals, distinguished people and their disciples. There were familiar New Testament images. The characters lived, for example, near a lake, a country residence to which they loved to escape from the hectic demands of the city: Jerusalem versus Galilee. The killing of the seagull introduces the idea of anger and unnecessary suffering, if not sacrifice. There is the single-minded 'innocence', idealism and enthusiasm of youth versus the traditionalism and monotony of experience. So what happens if you take these emotions, so powerful in the New Testament, and put scripture and drama side by side so that they can speak to each other?

Since most people will be unfamiliar with the play, it is important to clarify the story line, but if we are to avoid telling the story, making a prosaic comparison and then pointing a moral, we need to find a way of telling it which will enable the hearer to move once again within two worlds at the same time. There are two ways of doing this. One is to provide the setting and erect the signposts so that the hearers not only know where we are going but feel within themselves that this is a journey they want to make. They need to be comfortable with it. They may be part-way there already, but have never had the courage to go the whole way, or feel that if they travel it yet again, this time with Chekhov and the New Testament, they may see it all in a fresh light. The other approach is to choose words and images so carefully that the listeners have an experience of each world lighting up the other, both to their own personal advantage.

If we begin with the text, 'Jesus said to them, Follow me and I will make you become fishers of men,'[9] the biblical setting is clear, and the setting for the congregation may be to raise the question as to what it is that kicks a person off into Christian discipleship, and then (in some cases) into Christian ministry. That will grab some, as they think of their own experience and then of others they know. But quickly the question may be widened so as to bring in the rest. What is it indeed that kicks any of us off into the whole business of living? Obviously we don't know, any more than we know what it was that led these first four fishermen to drop their nets and to follow Jesus. But somewhere in the mixture it has something to do with ideals.

Ideals are usually associated with a person. A young girl with a potential for the stage is spurred on into acting because of some great actress she admires. (A description of Nina which will become more meaningful later!) A young fellow is drawn into business because he is captivated by the business tycoon who lives next door. Many a person drawn into the ministry is there because at some point in their experience he or she 'fell in love' with a 'successful' minister. It is our dreams and ideals related to people that keep us going. But if it is the having of ideals that gets us going, just as often it is the shattering of those ideals that brings us to despair, and that is how it was with Nina.

Nina is young and full of idealism. She lives in the country by a lake where she potters contentedly like the fishermen on the Sea of Galilee. But there is a man in her life by the name of Tregorin who comes down from the big city for periods of retreat, and he is burdened with success as a writer. Nina believes she is in love with him, though she is probably more in love with his fame and success than she is with him as a person. All the same there is a mutual attraction – Tregorin to Nina because he has forgotten what it is like to be young and therefore the girls in his stories are artificial, and Nina to Tregorin because she longs to be famous.

In one scene Nina talks to Tregorin about his fame and discovers to her horror that he rejects all claim to greatness and then goes on to talk about his life. It isn't at all what Nina imagined. Nina thinks his life is beautiful. Tregorin says it is nothing of the sort; he's just obsessed with the idea that he must write and he can't do anything else. Every time he finishes a work and is about to relax, a new idea grips him, and every time he sees something in the street, he has to make a note of it to work it into one of his stories somewhere. 'But you do have moments when you feel inspired,' says Nina, her ideal refusing to be shattered. 'Oh yes!', he agrees. He enjoys writing. And then the public read it and they say, 'It's very good, but it's not like Tolstoy.' Still hanging on, Nina tries to tell him that he's spoiled by success, and the blow falls. 'What success?' he says. And the rest of the speech shows how in his own estimation he has always felt a failure.

For the Ninas of life it is very hard to come to terms with the fact that what they had always thought was success was not really success at all, and that what they had always dreamed of as fame turns out to be an empty shell. She was not the first to have sat by a lake and gone through that experience. And Tregorin was not the first man to have to sit by a lake and disillusion those who had placed so much trust and confidence in him. Jesus was neither the son nor the brother his family would have liked him to be, and when they came to see him, they showed little understanding of the nature of his calling. No more was he the hero his disciples thought they had hitched themselves to. Suffering, passive resistance and rejection were not part of their agenda, so they quarrelled on the road to Jerusalem, fell asleep in the Garden of Gethsemane, produced a sword when it was the last thing he wanted, and with one exception were incapable of staying anywhere near the scene of action without losing their reputation. He certainly hadn't made much of an impact in the popularity stakes with the religious leaders, and any success he had with the crowds quickly evaporated under pressure. The gap between the hero and the worshipper could hardly be wider, and if the hero has difficulty conveying how he really feels to the worshipper then the worshipper has even more difficulty hearing it.

Yet both Jesus and Tregorin were undoubtedly successful, each in his own way, only for them success was not bright lights, fame or widespread recognition. Success in a way was not knowing how successful they were. And that idea opens up a whole new wave of understanding on the subject of ideals. It may stem from the fact that too many of us just plainly have the wrong ideals, but it is creative, positive and hopeful because it suggests that some of the most important and valuable things we do are the things of which we are least aware.

Most preachers can convey this from their own experience. They know how easy it is to list their achievements. They also know how when they return to the scene of former labours and talk to people, the things the people remember them for are very different from what they imagined. 'But when . . . (did I do this for you)?' is the question they want to ask. 'Amazing what people remember,' they say. 'I had no idea!' And if the recollections at this point are human and personal, members of the congregation will have little difficulty identifying with the experience; it is their experience too.

The problem, however, is not so much identifying the experience or even appreciating it; it is what it does to your former dreams and long-established ideals. If Jesus is right, then the disciples have got it wrong. And the discovery of the truth about Tregorin is a bitter blow to Nina. Like too many others before and after her, she can only handle her emotions by convincing herself that her idol has got feet of clay. Perhaps it is age, perhaps it is pressure from others. But he has lost his ideals. And instead of addressing her own problem she storms off with the all too familiar response, 'This is never going to happen to me.'

In that spirit she decides to become the actress she has always dreamed of being, and a regular mess she makes of it. And now it gets really hard. It is one thing to see your ideal not working for your idol; but how do you come to terms with the fact that it isn't working for you either? A few carefully chosen 'fallen idols' or 'shattered ideals' would very readily touch chords or ring bells for many hearers. But is this the point of greatest despair or is it the moment of hope? And is it because we have so few willing sacrifices that we also have so few resurrections?

There is certainly much in the experience of Tregorin that will appeal to many a preacher in middle to late life, and it may be no bad thing to share it with the congregation, if only to let them know that ministers and clergy too have their frustrations and disappointments. Every preacher begins with his dreams and ideals. They know who it is that they serve and who they want to follow. One may know roughly where he wants to be by the time he is fifty and what he wants to be doing, yet too many know that by that stage either the dream has faded or the focus has shifted. Drawing in the vast congregation has become preaching to the faithful few. Exploring exciting ideas and stimulating people by preaching and writing has become bashing away at a typewriter and nearly always being disappointed with it. Caring for people's pastoral needs has become listening to the same boring stories over and over again. The excitement of the sacrament has become routine. Leadership has become hours of hard labour persuading people to accept something, to do something or to change something which to you seemed so obviously right from the beginning. But is this failure which has to be accepted or opportunity which has to be grasped?

Jesus and the resurrection clearly supply one answer, but not necessarily one that everyone can find it easy to identify with. Nina's response may help some of them, because when she has gone out and lost pretty well everything (including her idealism), she returns and plays out a final scene with a childhood friend, a boy called Kostia with whom once she had shared all those dreams. In it she says:

> I think I know now, Kostia, that what matters in our work – whether you act on the stage or write stories – what really matters is not fame or glamour, not the things I used to dream about – but knowing how to endure things. How to bear one's cross and have faith.

But it is too much for Kostia and he goes out and shoots himself.

If legend is to be believed, this is what Peter had to learn on the Appian Way. Success was not being a big name in the church – it was the monotonous job, and in the end sweating it out with others in the dark days of persecution. Not the accolade of leadership – no Emmis, no Oscars – but just keeping on in a rapidly changing situation, helping others to find their way through the wilderness.

Yet even that may still be the easy bit! Coming to terms with the fact that the price of endurance is the death of the dream is even harder. When Nina and Kostia were young and sharing their ideals, Kostia came in one day with a seagull which he had shot and threw it at her feet. It became a symbol for Nina. When she was away and she wrote home she used to sign herself 'Seagull'. She saw herself very much as an idealist flying round the lake with her dreams. Shades again of the disciples with Jesus. And when she went out to fulfil those dreams in the big wide world, they were soon riddled with lead and they died. Yet it was in their death that Nina found life.

For many of us the temptations are too strong. We can never surrender that early vision, those dreams and ideals that got us going. We fly with them contentedly round the lake, where it's safe. We fear to launch out into the world because we know that out there there is a man with a gun who will easily reduce them to dust. He can make us a failure like the ones who have gone before, and we have a horror of becoming just like everybody else. *We* are different. *Our* dream must never die.

But Nina shows us that those who love their life will lose it, and those who hate their life in this world will keep it for eternal life.[10] So Peter turns on his heels and goes back to Rome. And Judas, unable to die, can only commit suicide. Jesus, for both, is the touchstone – he is either the rock on which our life is grounded, or the rock that falls on us and grinds us to dust. Nina went one way. Kostia went the other. Peter went one way, Judas went the other. We stand on the threshold. The door stands open. In the entrance is a God who is looking for seagulls.

Candle in the Wind

Candle in the Wind is a good example of what happens when you bring together a popular song,[11] a play[12] and a widely recognized Christian symbol in a very materialistic world where power is strength, the weak go to the wall and what matters most is 'the bottom line'.

If we are to begin where we are, the starting point might be that there is a touch of the candle about us all. The candle, like the human individual, is the one sure light in a crisis situation, but at the same time it is of all lights the most vulnerable. We are all of us so easily hurt. A harsh word, at a moment when our skin is tender, and we feel the wound for days. Even a glance from some people, and we spend all our dinner hour wondering what it meant. Nor are the tough characters, with faces like flint, exempt. Very often, under that harsh exterior, there is a heart so sensitive that it can only survive beneath rock.

Like a candle, too, we are victims of the wind and rain. Even a gentle wind, like a suggestion as to how we should dress, think or behave, will blow us in that direction. Give us a tough voice, a few orders, a couple of sanctions and one or two threats, and like a gust of wind or a shower of rain it will nearly snuff us out. 'We live our lives like a candle in the wind – and who are we to cling to when the rain sets in?' (Elton John).

By this point most of the congregation can identify. This is beginning to be *their* story. Time therefore to change the scene and direct their attention somewhere else, but not to anything very different, or we may lose them. Perhaps something with which they are familiar, but which they have not previously seen in this context.

In the New Testament, for example, we have a girl like this.[13] She is a slave with some peculiar mental disorder that makes her useful as a medium or a fortune-teller. A group of men, seeing an opportunity to make a little on the side, take her over as a candle and exploit her until she no longer exists as herself but only as their tool. She is the instrument to line their pockets. Their defence is that people like what she has to offer and are happy to pay for it, and she herself has never had it so good. (The language may lead some people to begin to put names to the description.)

But then this is how Elton John sees Marilyn Monroe,[14] and the song is not really a sympathetic concern for the weak, as I have been using the phrase, but an attack on a society that set her on the treadmill and made her change her name, thus turning a real person into a sex kitten for the sheer entertainment of others. To that extent she is more like the girl in the New Testament. Hollywood created a superstar, he says, and pain was the price she paid, so that even when she died a tragic death, the Press still hounded her, and all they could say was that 'Marilyn was found in the nude'. It is never difficult at this point to mention briefly one or two contemporary examples and question how many people even stop, like Elton John or Paul and Silas, simply to ask what society is doing to its weak and flickering candles.

On the contrary, there are usually far too many forces too busy 'trimming the wicks'. Was it really concern to soothe Saul that led those around him to engage David to play the harp, or was it rather that once Saul stopped having his successes they decided that the Spirit of the Lord had gone and a demon had taken over?[15] 'I am afraid he is not very well' is an oft-heard cry when a person suddenly fails or refuses to deliver. Candles need to be 'doctored' so that they glow in the right direction. It happens to politicians, to sports people and to many others, even in the church.

So where are we to find the defenders of the candle? Solzhenitsyn's *Candle in the Wind* does just that, but also demonstrates how often for those with the best intentions things have a way of going wrong. Two men, Alex and Philip, meet after years of separation. Philip began life as a philosopher and became a scientist. Alex began as a scientist, but a decade of internment in Desert California for a crime he didn't commit turned him into a philosopher. Philip loves this world's goods and everything science can provide, being held back only by an invalid wife who is incurable. Alex has had his own suffering, distrusts the science he once believed in so enthusiastically, and has discovered what are really Christian values,[16] though they are not called such. When they meet, Philip persuades Alex to go and work with him in his laboratory to pick up the threads.

Alex has a cousin called Alda, who embodies all his new-found values. She is something of a scatter-brain, but a delightful character, somewhat akin to nature; a true individualist but very sensitive. She cowers when a jet goes overhead and she jumps when a train roars by!

Alex and Philip decide to use her in an experiment to stabilize her, and Alex has the job of persuading her to agree, but there is no drama here, because it is clear from the beginning that she is the sort of person who can be persuaded very easily.[17] Alex knows this and does have some hesitation, but only when it is too late, and he says to Philip, 'She's a little candle, Philip! She's a little flickering candle in our terrible wind! Perhaps I was wrong to bring her here? Don't blow her out! Don't harm her!'[18]

The experiment is a success, but in stabilizing her they very nearly destroy her, and the last half of the play shows the effect of 'trimming the wick'. They have crushed the soul – because that is what the candle is – and they have destroyed her feelings. She doesn't cry at movies any more! And now she can describe how a bus ran over a dog, in great detail and without any feeling at all.[19]

But this is life, and up to this point the force of the song, the sermon and the drama will depend on the extent to which the preacher has managed first to capture the feelings of the congregation for the flickering candles and helped them to appreciate the risks to which such people are a prey in today's world. That in itself is a moment of judgment, as it leads the listeners to consider where they are themselves and who is around them. But in this instance the purpose is not so much to bring judgment or to achieve a different social attitude as to bring hope. Some of the listeners are after all candles themselves, and self-pity is not going to do them much good. It is worth asking, therefore, where in this situation we may find Christ.

Could it be in another character of whom we are scarcely aware, Aunt Christine? For the most part she never appears; she is only talked about, and she is a funny old lady. The rich relatives in fact make it clear that they know nothing about her at all. The only one who has any contact with her is Alda, but Alda says she lives in a hut with an earth floor, where the stove smokes and the roof leaks. Her life is looking after cats. She doesn't collect them, they come to her. Cats mutilated by naughty children – burned with kerosene, made to swallow pins, and with their paws cut off. And Aunt Christine lives for them. She only appears when her wealthy, gourmet, possession-conscious brother dies. She comes in, dressed in rags and carrying a bundle, makes the sign of the cross and reads the scriptures: 'Take heed that the light in thee be not darkness.'[20]

What such a combination of song, drama and scripture might achieve it is impossible to say, but hopefully it would make everyone more concerned for the protection of the weak, not only for the 'names' (the Marilyn Monroes of life) but also for the Aldas – the quiet, happy, simple, unassuming folk who are the victims of advertising, pressure groups and sometimes bossy relatives. If the light that is in us is the human soul, or the divine spark, then we need inspiration to protect the most vulnerable. But perhaps also the sermon would help some to spot a few more Aunt Christines and appreciate their worth. They may be odd and they may be peculiar, and the rich and the comfortable may choose to ignore them – but they may also be the very ones who make it possible for each candle to glow, and to give light to all who are in the house. And it may be a warning to others, lest they only recognize the value of Aunt Christine when they face the ultimate.

Which of these objectives is achieved will depend to some extent on the way the preacher has used and angled the material, but if it can be kept open, objective and balanced, the chances are that the Spirit will speak to people in different ways. That is what we should be after. We may not be able to command the Spirit, but we can at least make plenty of room for him.

4

Going on From Here

Among the tributes paid to Arthur Miller on his eightieth birthday was one from fellow-playwright David Mamet.[1] He said that he told Miller after *Death of a Salesman* that he felt as if he had been watching his own story – 'that you had written the story of my father and me – don't you think that strange?' Mamet then continued,

> I saw a small courteous smile on his face that said he did not find my remark strange at all – that, on the contrary, he had heard it from the vast majority of men who had seen the play and offered him a comment on it – that our response to a work of genius on the stage is: 'That is my story – not only did you write it about me, but I could go up on stage right now and act it.' Audiences in China said the same. 'That is the story of my father and me. We all stole the fountain pens. None of us won the football game. It was our story *and we did not know until we heard it*' (Italics mine).

The reaction is not unlike that of many people in the shanty towns of South America who found that when they came to read the story of the exodus, in their own language, especially if they were reading it for the first time, far from being preoccupied with questions of Egypt and the Nile and the miraculous crossing of the Red Sea, they did not even have to make the jump over 4000 years; they read it and simply said, 'This is our story'.

At this point Miller and his colleagues join hands with the liberation theologians, for they too are saying that what matters is the starting place – where we are and the context in which we are working – and that the objective in reading the Bible (or the drama) is not to interpret the Bible (or the drama) but to interpret life with the help of the Bible, because its meaning is not in the text but in the effect on the people reading it.[2] It gives them a new way of seeing, new eyes; and with that a new sense of reality. 'We are Abraham,' they say, 'We are in Egypt.' Carlos Mesters suggests that we need to think of the Bible more as 'history' and 'mirror' and less as 'letter' and 'symbol', because 'the common people are using it as a mirror to comprehend their own lives as a people'.[3] And when it comes to checking our interpretation for credibility, reliability and validity, then the test has to be, 'Do you see the signs of the kingdom? Do the blind see, can the lame walk, are the lepers cleaned, do the deaf hear, are the dead raised and do the poor have the good news preached to them?' (Luke 7.22).

Preaching that is to make something happen must continually explore new ways of combining the insights of the playwright and the liberation theologian so as to bring the hearers to the point where they say, 'This is my story – I could go up on stage right now and act it,' even if they did not know it was their story 'until they heard it'. But how?

Just as every person has to discover his or her own story, because it is theirs and nobody's else's, so in the same way all preachers have to discover their own individual styles and methods. Hopefully what has been written thus far, some of it in great detail and all of it seen very much through one man's eyes, may be sufficient to enable readers to find themselves – to see *their* own story! What follows is intended simply to sketch out a few ideas and notions which may be worth exploring, and this explains the change of style. Much, though not all, is similar to what I have expressed more fully in the earlier chapters. Some ideas are fairly well developed. Others are deliberately sketchy. Some readers may need more than others, but from this point all readers or preachers are on their own. They may all start in the same place. No two are likely to finish in the same place.

The Bible

Bearing in mind what I said earlier about the prophets, especially Micah and Hosea,[4] it may be worth trying to apply something of the same method to others. Here are some 'starters', followed by some 'seed thoughts' on Bible story-telling.

Ezekiel

On the Sunday before Advent the Common Lectionary,[5] under the theme, 'Christ the King', prescribes Ezekiel 34.1–17, Psalm 23, I Corinthians 15.20–28 and Matthew 25.31–46 as the readings for Holy Communion. In fifteen minutes there is scant hope of doing justice to all four passages, but with Christmas in everybody's mind, and knowing that even as early as this (with school plays in the offing), somebody somewhere is sure to be asking questions about the nativity stories, try bringing together 'Ezekiel and the Shepherds'.[6]

Set the scene by placing Psalm 23, so familiar as not to be noticed, and so often sentimentalized as to be barely recognizable by a real shepherd, side by side with a reading from the life of a real shepherd today.[7]

Capture the imagination with a picture of rural England as we all imagine it – village fête, Harvest Home and the smell of new-mown hay – compared to today, followed by a second paragraph showing how the spirit that led the shepherd to care for the sheep once also led the community to care for one another, thus bridging the gap between then and now. Many people will soon feel that something has gone wrong. In Ezekiel's case (sticking closely now to the biblical text), the problem is that the carers don't care, and if God has had enough of them they should know why. So where had they gone wrong?

Answers are set out in vv.1–6. Those responsible for others are helping themselves. The natural life of the sheep is being interfered with. Left to themselves, with the minimum of caring, a little pasture and freedom to roam, the sheep will get on with the job – they will give good milk, wool and meat. But these shepherds are not satisfied. So they consume the milk, wear the wool and even slaughter the fat beasts, but they don't actually feed the flock (v.3). You could say that they 'milk the sheep, fleece the flock and strip their assets without any long-term care or investment'. If the scene has been carefully set, and the community are feeling let down by their leaders, something may quickly begin to happen.

Reflect further on what it might be, with one eye on the sheep and the other on contemporary society. Choose your method. One way is to pick out three or four stories from the week's press where carers are making impossible demands and at the same time obviously helping themselves rather than caring for the sheep. Such incidents are not usually difficult to find. They touch people on issues where they are already concerned and stimulate them to examine more carefully what is going on.

A more subtle way might be to choose language applicable to both worlds in such a way that each hearer can take it straight or read between the lines. To achieve this, sharpen in your mind exactly what happened. For example, to begin with, the harsh treatment seemed to work. Of course, a few weak sheep couldn't cope, some showed signs of weariness, some got hurt, some fell sick, some just fell behind and some went plain astray, but everybody knew that was to be expected. The wilderness is a tough place for tender lambs to grow up in.

In the same vein, notice how though at first a few of the more caring shepherds no doubt saw what was happening and drew attention to it, most of the shepherds were actually better off, so nothing happened (vv.2,8), until even the caring shepherds learned to live with the situation and to pretend it wasn't happening at all. The result was that in the end even the strongest sheep – 'driven with ruthless severity' – couldn't take it (vv.4–5 REB).

No wonder God gave up on those shepherds and took the law into his own hands! But who is Ezekiel? And is he still with us? And is the Word still alive among us?

Time perhaps to change the tempo. What happens when you turn to 'another sheep story' (Matt. 25) and interpret it as a parable of judgment rather than a moral about caring – sorting out the flock? It may spring some surprises.

You might ask why we have so little time for those shepherds who were on the make in Ezekiel. Could it be that we assume we do not belong to them? 'They' are always somebody else. Never us! Matthew 25 sings a different tune. It shouts aloud that those who think they are 'in' may very well find they are 'out', and calls us to remember that if we like to think of ourselves as shepherds, even only 'as one who cares' or is 'concerned', we too stand under that same judgment.

A few pertinent reminders may serve to bring this home. Structures, even caring structures (perhaps especially caring structures!), possibly even structures we are personally involved in, often on examination show themselves to be surprisingly cleverly structured for the benefit of those who belong to them. Few 'carers' find it easy to listen to their customers (clients). Few professionals can face the thought of their professional pyramid being turned upside down. Shades of Ezekiel and a God who intervenes to take control?

Finally, to keep things earthed in the present, does this have something to say to us about the sort of shepherd we ought to be thinking about at Christmas? Not perhaps the sentimental nocturnal visit, with the ox and the ass and the smell of the straw, but the real struggle of the shepherd in Psalm 23, Ezekiel 34 and Matthew 25. Of course this could spoil somebody's Christmas Day, but it could also make them a much fitter and healthier person on Boxing Day, and if it did that, something really would have happened.

Jeremiah

One of the basic tasks of the prophet, like that of the preacher, was to help people make sense of what was going on and to give them hope. Jeremiah 32.15[8] provides a good text for a prophet whose life was committed perhaps more than most to 'Making Sense of It'.

Begin the sermon with the idea that this is the sort of text everybody wants to hear. It spells hope. But then to appreciate what it means, describe the situation facing the exiles, with one eye on Jeremiah and the other eye on Britain's increasing feelings of threat from Europe. Paint a picture of what it means to see all that you have inherited and built up over 500 years beginning to fall apart – your natural leaders about to be whisked off to another country, no Empire, no sovereignty, no government, no defences, no currency and so on, with some leaders actually arguing that the new alliance may be all for the best. Not exactly the time to buy a house or take out a long-term investment! Imagine the fall-out if the nasty dream came true. Use Psalm 137 to help to bring out the emotions. Touch the nerve of a people who feel that life is raw, if not over.

Then turn to Jeremiah. Unlike some of the other prophets who were moved by exploitation, social and moral injustice, or the plight of the poor, Jeremiah sees his role in terms of explaining and defending the ways of God to men. In a tough situation he has to make sense of it. He does so in two ways.

First, he buys a field. In a day of total darkness, he thinks he can see a glimmer, but can anybody be that daft? Imagine meeting him in the local park. Does he think things are looking up? 'No. Disaster is round the corner. Our rulers have got it all wrong. We never ought to be contemplating these foreign alliances. Our strength lies not in lining up with everybody else but in God and in loyalty to him alone.' So why this long-term investment? Because much as he dislikes what is going on, he can still believe that under God it will provide a platform for a new day and a new nation.

To help people to feel what is happening, and keeping close to the text, use the very pictures Jeremiah paints, and paint one or two contemporary pictures of your own. People returning to towns they were forced to leave and hearing again the sound of music and laughter (Bosnia? Belfast?). The renewal of the countryside (Grass growing on the motorways? The environment?). Avoid nostalgia. Jeremiah knows his sufferings are not over. The worst is still to come. But God is in control. And long before the resurrection, Jeremiah had a pretty good idea what it was all about.

So is Jeremiah's message 'Back to basics and traditional values'? Religion even? Not exactly. Certainly not religion written on tablets of stone. More of a new covenant, written in the hearts of the people and expressed in personal integrity. And that's Jeremiah's second contribution: basic integrity. Compare him with Hananiah, his chief antagonist, who had picked up the language of political correctness and who cried 'Peace, peace' when (in Jeremiah's book) there was no peace.

Finally, focus on someone doing just that in today's world, preferably someone much appreciated for professionalism but whose message many people would willingly suppress.[9] And conclude with that covenant waiting to be written on our hearts and the assertion that as long as there is only one person prepared to give his or her life for a better future when all is black, there is hope. Let people feel it, and send them out with the word,

> 'This could be just the moment to go and buy that field and plant those trees. In twenty years somebody may thank you.'

Isaiah 6

A useful starting point is to bring together a Bible passage and a contemporary event in such a way as to enable one to 'speak' to the other, allowing each to plumb the depths of the other so that the hearers can sense the relevance of something that happened 2,000 years ago to something in their experience without the preacher having to engage in a double hermeneutic.

Next time Isaiah 6 comes up, for example therefore, try putting it side by side with an experience of Nelson Mandela[10] to see if together they help the congregation to recognize similar experiences in their own life and to work out what it means to be called.

Isaiah's call is that of a man conscious of living in two worlds. At one level it is the world of sin and holiness, and he feels the need to be cleansed from one in order to enter the other. But at another level it is the world to which he belongs and the new world to which he feels called. In a similar way Mandela was a child of two worlds.

Of his earthly parentage and the ordinariness of his early years there could be no doubt. He knew what it was to run barefoot in the village with the other boys, to share their pleasures, games, hopes, fears, disappointments and natural naughtiness, and his recent recollections of those early years are ample evidence of the extent to which he enjoyed them.

But then, at the age of nine, following the death of his father, he was sent away to live with Chief Jongintaba, acting regent of the Thembu people, who was to be his guardian and benefactor for the next decade, in return for services rendered to him by

Mandela's father. From now on Mandela was to be groomed for
education and privilege; doors were to be opened to higher
education and the legal profession, where a black lawyer was still
such a rarity that some whites refused even to recognize him.
With privilege went responsibility. Slowly he had to learn
obedience, and so it was that he developed (often in the hard way)
a sense of his own personal commitment and integrity. Hitherto
church and religion had not meant much to him, but now he
discovered what happened when you put yourself first. This was
also where he learned democracy. When the regent and his court
met, all the Thembus were allowed to come, whether the item on
the agenda was a drought, the culling of cattle, policies ordered
by a magistrate or new laws decreed by government. Not only
were all free to come, they were also free to speak, and all were
heard. The regent himself was not above criticism, and the
meetings went on until consensus was reached. 'Majority rule
was a foreign notion. A minority was not to be crushed by a
majority' (p.20).

At one level the experience of both men was simply that of
growing up and learning to take responsibility for their own life
and for the lives of others. That immediately gives the parallel a
broader reference. The experience is a common one. At another
level it is the regular and continuing experience of everyone who
matures with life. Life is a matter of constantly learning to die to
one world in order to live to another; it is learning to get a true
perspective on life so as to know what has to be abandoned and
what has to be retained. And at yet a third level (to go no further)
it is a unique experience which comes to many people, some of
whom would describe it as a conversion and others as a call. You
might select a number of contemporary stories to demonstrate
some or all of these experiences, so as to enable the hearer to
identify with both Isaiah and Mandela.

But then came the crunch experience for both of them. The
Isaiah story is familiar. Mandela's must be described in some
detail. It was in his final year at school that something happened
which he describes as 'like a comet streaking across the night
sky'.[11] They had a visit from the great Xhosa poet, Krune
Mqhayi, who entered the hall in full tribal dress with a spear in

each hand. Mandela finds it hard to explain the impact made by a black man so dressed entering the hall through that door in that way. 'It seemed to turn the universe upside down.'[12] A thunder-bolt? But then when he spoke, Mandela at first was disappointed. Mqhayi seemed to have difficulty finding the right words. Then all at once he raised his assegai into the air for emphasis and accidentally hit the curtain. The poet looked at his spear, then at the curtain, walked back and forth across the stage, and all at once became energized. He said that the assegai striking the curtain rail symbolized the clash between the culture of Africa and that of Europe:

> 'The assegai stands for what is glorious and true in African history, it is a symbol of the African as warrior and the African as artist. This metal wire,' he said, pointing above, 'is an example of western manufacturing, which is skilful but cold, clever but soulless.'

Mandela says that he could hardly believe his ears. Not only did this arouse and motivate him, but it also gave him a new perception of his white, English headmaster, who until then he had always automatically considered his benefactor. And when Mqhayi went on to recite his well-known poem in which he apportions the stars in the heavens to the various nations of the world and got to the point where he reserved the most important and transcendent star, 'the Morning Star', for the Xhosa people, the deal for Mandela was clinched. 'I felt like one of the chosen people.' He knew now who he was and what he had to do.

It is of course impossible to prescribe any outcome to a sermon on these lines, but if the preacher has done enough homework both on the text and on Mandela, and has carefully harnessed the fundamental human experience in the middle section to the lives of the hearers, it is hard to think that nothing would happen, particularly if the sermon could be written in such a way as to move imperceptibly from one world to the other.

Storytelling

I referred earlier to skill with narrative and short stories, like 'The Bag Lady',[13] and we will return to the subject later.[14] However, before we leave the Bible, it is worth noting the trend, and cultivating the habit of presenting material in the form of a short story in such a way as to bring out a significance which might otherwise be missed. One writer who had made his own contribution to this in recent years is Trevor Dennis.

His collection of stories, *Speaking of God*, provides several examples which, whilst particularly appropriate for those required to preach shorter sermons, also contains insights for those who want to incorporate a few 'catchy tunes and rhythms' into their more elaborate symphonies and concertos. There is the story of God's laughter, leading to the remark that 'he came to teach his world to laugh';[15] of Eve telling Adam (though not with those names) that Adam would never be content in the garden as long as 'he' (God) was there because Adam would want to make it his own;[16] the bringing together of Abraham's sacrifice of Isaac and Golgotha;[17] the linking of stories from the Gospels with stories from children's literature;[18] the God who died in the crush of a stadium disaster;[19] the God who is to be found only in the crying;[20] and the child who senses the presence of the Creator in a flock of dunlin, relates it to Moses shielding his eyes with his hand when he senses God in the cleft of a rock,[21] and then sharply reproves the adult for trying to identify him and so capture him, with the words:

> He is the flock, and he hides himself in the flock. He is most elusive, and he is there plain for you to see. He is most insignificant, yet he makes all divine.[22]

Each in its own way is capable of making something happen that may not form part of the preacher's plan or intentions and is certainly not within the preacher's control, but which nevertheless opens up the possibility of a fresh approach. Several of Dennis's stories, when combined with other biblical passages, stories from literature or contemporary material, will provide an excellent basis for a richer and more fully-developed sermon.[23]

Begin with the idea of laughter,[24] for example, and relate it to Sarah's laughter,[25] to bring out the different kinds of laughter and the power of laughter. Identify two kinds of people – those who can only laugh once they escape from a tough situation and those who can laugh inside a tough situation in order to handle it, the clown and the satirist. Look at the people who laugh a lot, and try to find out why. Ask yourself who you can laugh with. Read Harry Williams's description of the experience of the Delectable Mountains in *Pilgrim's Progress* as 'the laughter of heaven'[26] and relate it to 'elements of a practical joke' in Alwyn Marriage's interpretation of Palm Sunday,[27] or explore Jewish humour[28] to discover how Jewish humour actually succeeds in using the victim to change the perception, just as Jesus on the cross (God's Fool?[29]) changed the perception of the world for all time. And for those who have difficulty with theology, read *The Herries Chronicle*[30] and find out what Vanessa says at the end to a friend who asks her why she loves Benjie so much when life with him is so tortuous.

In another book,[31] Dennis combines the skill of the preacher and the authority of the Old Testament teacher to encourage us to make much greater use of the Old Testament which is so rich in story material, much of which has the advantage that it does not demand an enormous amount of background material before we begin. Instead of *looking at* the text he invites us to an *engagement with* the text, to use our imagination and emotions and to allow ourselves to be 'excited by it, amused by it, disturbed by it'.[32] Here too the story may be allowed to speak for itself and say what it wants to say within the given context. However, that does not mean we should not use other aids occasionally, not in order to make the story say what we *want* it to say, but to enable the questions which it raises to come through and demand an answer.

One example is the way in which Dennis analyses the two gifts of manna and quails (Ex. 16 and Num. 11).[33] He asks why it is that in Exodus God replies to complaints with 'miracles of salvation' whereas in Numbers God responds with 'miracles of devastating destruction', and then goes on to show how Sinai made all the difference. True, the result is essentially cerebral, and there is nothing here along the lines of 'making something happen', but his capacity to tell the story in a different way opens up new possibilities from which the preacher may go further.

Or take 'A Wrestling Match with God', based on the story of

Jacob and Esau (Gen. 32–33).[34] Here again the story is put in a
wider setting and there is a section on 'making sense of God'[35]
which concludes with the cross and describes God's wrestling
match as a tale which 'can take us to the very summit of Calvary,
and deep into the still broken heart of God'.[36] It is 'the scandal of
particularity'. Why should God choose this nation and not that,
this family and not that, even this brother and not that?

There is a passing reference to Cain and Abel[37] which is then
worth exploring further, if only because there is so much
interesting biblical and extra-biblical material on the story in
Genesis 4. What happens, for example, when you bring together
one or more of the various interpretations of Genesis 4,[38] the
treatment of Cain and Abel by John Steinbeck,[39] the different
interpretations of Steinbeck in film,[40] and then put that side by
side with Jacob and Esau so as to lead up to the cross (à la
Dennis)? Or when you put the stories side by side with Willy
Russell's 'rags to riches' story, *Blood Brothers*, which explores
what happens when twin brothers are brought up in totally
different environments because one of them is given away at birth
by his mother (Mrs Johnstone, a charlady who already has more
children than she can cope with), to Mrs Lyons for whom she
works and who begs for him at birth. The two boys grow up
streets apart, never learning the truth, but becoming firm friends
(even in love with the same girl) despite their different backgrounds and the attempts of Mrs Lyons to keep them apart. One
goes to the local comprehensive, the other to public school. In
school holidays they meet and play together with all kinds of
consequences, but still without knowing they are brothers. Then
Mickey Johnstone loses his job, marries the girl, turns to crime
and becomes dependent on tranquillizers, whilst Edward Lyons
prospers, goes to university and becomes a councillor, and so on.
In the end the truth has to come out, and the curtain comes down
with a line that leaves you breathless.

To gain force, make it clear early on whose needs are to be
addressed that day. It could be those who feel that they are on the
wrong side of every counter, that what they have to offer has
never been wanted or acceptable, and that when they open their
lips to speak somebody always get in before them. They may

never understand why Cain's sacrifice was unacceptable (and would it matter if they did?), but they certainly know what it feels like. Steinbeck helps to sketch in the possibilities. Russell supplies experiences. The lame man by the Pool of Bethesda[41] adds a biblical dimension. Reasons, arguments and explanations are irrelevant. What these people need to feel is how it makes all the difference to life when somebody stops by and notices them, or when they can see one of their number despised and rejected to the ultimate and yet making new life possible for others. Any sermon which can explore these various ideas so as to help people through that experience will be water in the desert to a thirsty soul.

Almost any one of Dennis's stories would spark off a preacher somewhere who wanted to break new ground, but their value lies not so much in the ideas or interpretations which he offers as in the style of writing. Nobody, of course, is going to write as Dennis writes, and nobody, one hopes, is going to use him as he is or even try and copy him, but there is much to be gained by reading him in order to discover one's own original way of producing similar material.

Life

Many sermons that originate in life experiences are of necessity personal. Like Amos, the preacher sees 'the basket of summer fruit' and spontaneously begins preaching about 'the end'.[42] For such sermons it is difficult to prescribe. But there are other experiences which are common to us all and which (like the poor) are always with us, such as our understanding of God, loneliness, isolation and justice (or injustice), how to survive in an impossible situation (like a hostage or an intolerable marriage or family relationship), race, colour and apartheid, nuclear deterrents and whether it is right to take up arms.

Here are five examples. How to raise questions about the nature of God, how to cope with the feeling that whatever you do you can never find God, how to respond when you are under pressure to the point of persecution, how to handle apartheid (not as a remote academic issue that affects others but as a highly relevant and emotional topic that affects us all and has not disappeared with the recent changes in South Africa), and how we treat people.

The nature of God

If a cruise in the Arctic led me to take a fresh look at the God of the Mountains,[43] perhaps a re-reading of T. S. Eliot's poem, 'The Naming of Cats',[44] enriched maybe by some of the music by Andrew Lloyd Webber, could help others to some aspects of God's character not normally considered.

The experience of Moses with the burning bush, when he feels called to deliver his people in the name of God but is unsure as to God's name, provides a useful biblical basis, leading as it does to the assertion, 'I am who I am'.[45] However, it may be better simply to begin by reading Eliot's poem and asking people to consider whether God might not be 'a cat' because God, too, has three different names.

To begin with, it may be necessary to establish the existence of 'different gods' (or at least different concepts of God) by showing how whenever and wherever we speak of God, we are not always speaking of the same being.[46] Even apart from the problems presented by the existence of other religions, is there not a difference between the God of the altar or the sacrament and the God of the Puritans or the Moral Majority? Or between the God we worship on Sunday and the God we worship the rest of the week? And are not all these gods 'different' from the God revealed to us in Jesus Christ? Was this not what Paul was reflecting when he wrote about 'principalities and powers' and 'the rulers of this world'?[47] This is the 'cat' by the name we all know and have no difficulty recognizing: the Deity, the Almighty, and so on. He is the God, in one form or another, to whom all humanity addresses its prayers.[48]

Secondly, paint a picture of the God who comes in Jesus Christ – the special name given to a particular cat because he was different, or what he did was different, from all the others. Bring out the way in which he had a different attitude on so many subjects from the faith in which he was brought up: a different attitude to Gentiles, to women, to the sick, to the poor and to the sinner. He was a regular attender at the temple, and yet never afraid to challenge the established faith of the fathers. The Magnificat, perhaps, affords a useful way of bringing together so many of these ideas, either directly in the sermon or indirectly at some other point in the service, but it is probably important to spell out that in no sense is this a 'different' cat (or God).

But then thirdly, explore the following lines in the light of the text:

> But above and beyond there's one name left over,
> And that is the name that you never will guess;
> The name that no human research can discover –
> But THE CAT HIMSELF KNOWS, and will never confess.

For many people this could well be the moment when something happens. All cat lovers know what it means in a way that dog lovers may find it difficult to appreciate, and the remaining lines of the poem bring it home even more, so while the iron is hot move towards the conclusion to demonstrate how Exodus 3.15 is making it clear beyond a peradventure that there is no way we can ever fully grasp who God is or what God does. Let it be a warning to those religious people who try (not to mention those who think they have succeeded!), and a word of comfort to those who find it difficult.

For many that will be enough. Preachers who want to take it further may go on to point out that to live with one of those names for God is to live with a very stunted and inadequate picture of the God who comes to us in Jesus Christ, or that the name you focus on most will determine the sort of person you become. Since by this stage many hearers will already have 'felt' (even if they have not consciously decided) which is most appealing to them, the next few moments when the different issues are brought out could be quite decisive. Are they satisfied with themselves or not?

To avoid any suggestion of 'loading' the argument, conclude with a story of how two or three different people responded to the same situation to bring out the differences, thus enabling each listener to become aware with whom they naturally identify. A useful resource here might be the film, *The Mission*, where in three figures you have the official church, a conforming priest and a rebel (also a priest). And which is the one who is responding to that 'deep and inscrutable singular name'?

O that I knew . . .

What are we to say to the people who regularly attend church but nevertheless live with the feeling that they can never quite find God in the way that (they imagine) others do? Is their problem the same as that of those who feel that they are the victims of injustice and there is nowhere they can press their case? Try exploring either or both these questions, separately or together, after reading Kakfa, *The Trial*.[49]

Possible scripture readings are Job 23.1–12 and John 20.24–29; 21.2–3, with a title such as 'Doors and Doorkeepers', the significance of which will be immediately apparent to anyone who has read the story.

Begin with a story or two from recent press and news reports of those who felt they were the victims of injustice and when they tried to present their case either there was nobody there, or they were there but didn't listen. Or there was simply no way to get through – only an effective doorkeeper to bar the way to legitimate justice. People's feelings about finding God are very similar.[50] For some people all the time and for everybody some of the time God and justice are just not there when they are wanted. Examples could be cited from scripture.

Briefly relate the story of *The Trial*. Bring out the agony of waiting, the frustration, the stress, the stupidity, the anger against the doorkeeper who is not really the cause of the problem, the imponderables beyond, and so on. Notice what it does to the victim and how it helps him in the end to realize that there are others whom he never sees but who are going through the same experience. Peel off the layers to the point where the congregation really feel the depths and desperately wait for the word of hope which they know every preacher must bring.

But then avoid it. Today's story is not for those who can always hope. It is for those who may never find it, or who certainly cannot find it just yet. For once at least, let it be a message for those who have to continue the struggle – for Job (1–37, not 38–42); for Thomas over a period of eight days; and for disciples who just have to go on fishing – because in times and places when all is lost and it seems as if God (or justice) no longer exist, then honesty and integrity compel us to come to terms with living as if they didn't.

Try to find someone who managed it. Perhaps someone listening will sense in them a hope that can only come alive in their own despair. Simone Weil, perhaps, of whom Joseph Donders[51] wrote that in France during the Second World War she became so tired of Christians and others praying for justice and peace while people were being persecuted and victimized and yet doing nothing to help their prayers to be heard

> . . . that she decided
> to live a life without that escape,
> to live as if God did not exist.

This does not mean that people will suddenly find the justice, health or faith they are looking for. But once they can accept the possibility of living without it, it might not matter – or at least it might not matter quite so much!

Civil disobedience

Civil disobedience is not what it used to be. Thanks to the more lurid tabloid descriptions of events at Aldermaston, Greenham Common and Twyford Down it used to be possible to dismiss it as something for the rebels and the trouble-makers. But as a result of more recent legislation it is just as likely to involve 'middle-class respectables'. Choose a few examples carefully to help the congregation to feel that civil disobedience nowadays is just as likely to involve 'us' as 'them', even if only as a whistle-blower or as one who feels compelled to put principle before precept, right before accepted codes of conduct. How are we to respond when doing what we feel in our bones to be right puts us under pressure to the point of persecution?

Biblical material is not lacking. Psalm 149 (especially the closing verses) seems to suggest that rebellion against unjust rulers is in order, though Romans 13 takes a different view of 'the governing authorities', whilst I Maccabees 2.29–38 and 39–48 demonstrate the price of conforming over against the price of rebellion. But the Book of Daniel perhaps provides the best background material to build up the case, deriving some of its strength from the fact that it already 'speaks' to two eras, fifth-century Babylon and second-century Hellenistic civilization.

In fifth-century Babylon you have Jews living in exile under a foreign power. Use the commentaries to paint the picture and use language that makes it sound contemporary. Some immigrants, for example, like Daniel, have done rather well. Perhaps too much so for the comfort of the locals. So 'the natives' want legislation to curb their progress. Not too much. That would be counter-productive. Just an edict here, an edict there and much of it temporary, and so on. But imagine the effect of even that on people who already feel that they have had to give up nearly everything that is precious to them. They are surrounded by an alien culture; they can't go out of their homes without hearing a foreign language, and many of them are openly abused.

In second-century Hellenistic Palestine the problem is more the change from a religious-based society to a secular one. The old controls were religious ones and people respected them even if they didn't keep them. The new ones were secular. The king was now taking the place of God.

Choose a number of examples of the same problems from contemporary society. Who today is feeling these pressures? Is it one group of people in both cases or is it two? Outline the issues in such a way that the hearers find it easy to identify with at least one group and then choose words to make them feel and think what they are doing about it, comparing it with what many of them probably think they ought to be feeling and doing. Help them to feel the force of the text to such an extent that Daniel's story becomes their story. Spare a thought, too, for the people caught in the crossfire. Some are fearful for their own skin, some are fearful for their families. But some are anxious because, however strongly they feel, civil disobedience is just something they cannot contemplate, even though they know that it is probably the only thing that will be effective.

How then can we present this in another context so that we can stand back from it and see ourselves?

I referred earlier[52] to Bonhoeffer's courage, first by trying to bring peace between Britain and Germany and then by taking part in the plot to assassinate Hitler. Another aspect of his life worth exploring is the way in which he handled the conflict between the very distinguished German family with a long line of public service to which he belonged and the realization that there might come a point where in order to be loyal to that distinguished line he might have to do something which to all his ancestors would have been anathema – a moment when he would have to appear to be disloyal to them in order to be loyal to himself. Reflect on his emotions as they come through in his well-known hymn,[53] or use some of the more popular and anecdotal material from the many Bonhoeffer books[54] to make his story come alive today.

Another, more contemporary, possibility is Ariel Dorfman's play, *Death and the Maiden,* which opens up issues of life and death in Chile under Pinochet in such a way that it is difficult for us not to see them, and yet relatively easy for us to dismiss them as somebody else's problem, and where there is music by Schubert and Mahler to help to create the atmosphere. But what is most powerful of all is the ending which blocks off all escape and compels us to see the play as a play not about 'them' but about 'us'. Would that every sermon could achieve that level of involvement, judgment and commitment!

Apartheid

On one occasion when my theme was to be 'Comfortable with Apartheid', it suddenly occurred to me that it might be improved if it were delivered as a short drama with five scenes and an interval. That structure could be worth trying.

Use Scene One to establish the concept of 'us and them' in a perfectly legitimate way, such as training young children to know whom they can and whom they must not trust, but then use other material to show how when we grow up this same concept becomes a very useful device for self-indulgence ('us' before 'them'), if not downright self-preservation ('me first'). Think of it in relation to 'NIMBY', 'get off my patch', 'buy foreign' (because it's cheaper), or 'Buy British' (regardless of what it does to the Third World). A society of sheep and goats – and we like it that way.

Use Scene Two to demonstrate what a marvellous concept that sinful idea is when you want to protect your religion. The evidence is endless, in every generation, and religious people thrive on it. We are insensitive to its dangers. We even go out of our way to reinforce it. (Don't *make* the point! Find the evidence in the press and simply remind people of what they know to be all around them. Putting it in this context will enable them to see it differently.) Indeed religion seems to find it difficult to live without some form of apartheid so that 'we' can be sheep and 'they' can be goats.

In Scene Three you might move out into the political arena, where the real horrors of apartheid reveal themselves. 'Us and them' is everywhere, and one current story should be adequate.

By now not more than twelve minutes should have passed. It has been getting worse all the time and people can stand no more. Time for a break. The interval. You might even leave the pulpit for sixty seconds to make a different point. Try reflecting (as one might in a theatre interval) on what 'that preacher up there' has just been saying. Ruminate on what happens, for example, when barriers come down. Shades of Eastern Europe. Racially mixed communities. Vatican II and church unity. Chaos and confusion rather than law and order! Fear rather than security! Open house with no checks and balances! This is a moment to ease the anxieties building up in the congregation at what you have said so far, and a moment to let them know that you are aware of how they are feeling. Then you are interrupted because 'the bell goes' and you return to the pulpit to continue the drama.

Scene Four is Jesus telling the story of the sheep and the goats. This is 'the religious bit'. (Convey the idea indirectly by describing the scene – churches, spires and domes, an open book, a cup and some bread, towel and basin, and a tree.) Then describe the reactions on the faces of the crowd. They love it. Good strong leadership. They are with him. *They* know the goats! Until suddenly they realize he isn't saying what they thought he was saying. One day they might be in for a shock. This is outrageous. One family? Don't judge? Wheat and tares growing together? Unity with that lot?

Scene Five and we are back where we are – in church. What are we to make of it? Try offering an alternative form of apartheid that we can be comfortable with – that between the redeemed and the unredeemed, where the unredeemed are those who say 'that's how it is and you can't do anything about it', and the redeemed are those who say 'that's how it is, but it doesn't have to be that way'. Ideally you then need one story where that works and with which the listener can identify. Marriage perhaps, or some other form of close relationship which you know would lead to the ultimate sacrifice.

Resurrection now

When people are having difficulty with the empty tomb, possibly because they find it a difficult concept, possibly because they doubt whether it ever happened in the way the New Testament stories suggest, or possibly because they feel that their faith requires something more than assent to the efficacy of a miracle 2000 years ago for today, how are we to help them to appreciate the resurrection as something that is happening all the time? One way is to put the idea in a different setting and take advantage of some insight from a prisoner of conscience.

Take Isaiah 40.5 as a text, but begin by exploring the feeling of living in a sewer. There are many levels. People living in the industrial areas of Britain in the 1930s felt as if they were living in a sewer. Paint a picture, possibly with the help of some of the literature from the period. Some people feel as if they are living in a sewer when they find themselves watching certain programmes on television. Some do when they read or see what goes on in Westminster, whether it be at the political level or the personal level. And, to keep the sermon biblical, read Isaiah 24.5 and remember this was how the scribes and

Pharisees felt only too often. John the Baptist voiced many of their emotions.

When people are able to identify with the experience, or perhaps begin to feel uncomfortable about it, try putting it side by side with a letter from a Dominican Brazilian priest, written just before Christmas 1970 whilst he was a prisoner of conscience, who really felt as if he were living in a sewer – literally! Forty or fifty of them were living in a cell that was none too large and none too healthy:

> Everything that society banishes from its midst ends up here. It's like a giant sewer into which refuse drains on its way to the ocean that is freedom. Living in a sewer is an undesirable experience. Here all sorts of cast-offs meet, both the bad and the good . . . we live together with the moles and cockroaches that breed under the city.[55]

But then, just when everybody is thinking how dreadful it must be, he goes on to describe how 'here underground great things are happening'. Down there in the darkness, seeds germinate. This is where you find the roots of the plants that will flower in the spring. This is where you find silver and gold, and the roots of ancient oak trees. This is where everything is born, blossoms and begins to rush towards the light.

From this moment there are at least two ways to go. One is to demonstrate that the whole business of living in a sewer is a matter of perception. You might cite one or two of the more grimy and seedy sides of life and go on to show how they too make their contribution for those who are prepared to look with the eye of faith. The other way is to unpack each of those phrases in the last paragraph (along with several more in the letter) and relate a story or an incident to demonstrate their truth. This really is life coming out of death . . . now!

But what makes the difference? The desert is still a desert. The sewer is still a sewer. Is it only a matter of perception? Of faith? The Dominican priest says no. Resurrection really does happen, because when you are at desperation point in the sewer the one thing you do is to join hands with your fellow sufferers, and it is in this comradeship that you find salvation.

As the hearer begins to sense the wonder it may be time to pop the question: could that be why we miss it? Resurrection doesn't come from nowhere. It doesn't just happen. It only comes from literally and physically going down into the depths and sharing in the sufferings of those at the bottom of heap. This is incarnation; joining hands and joining forces with the whole of the created order as it struggles towards the light. It leads to resurrection. And if we have difficulty experiencing it, could it be because we have been unwilling to face the darkness? Do we miss the resurrection because we have never really appreciated the incarnation? And if we could, might we have a better grasp of what it means for the glory of the Lord to be revealed so that all flesh will see it together?

Literature

Besides providing us with a wealth of material which we can use alongside the Bible and the experiences of life there are occasions, as we have seen, when a piece of literature can provide the basis for a whole discourse or indeed a series of discourses. Many of them are found by accident, though you may only notice them as a result of years of experience of asking questions and training your eyes to be observant. There are three stages. First, being gripped by something which seems important. Second, working out its theological or homiletical potential. Third, deciding how to relate it to scripture and the day-to-day experience of the congregation.

Sometimes it is good to begin the discourse with the literature and develop it, introducing scripture and contemporary experience as appropriate. Sometimes, having located the relevant scripture passage, it is good to begin there, using the literary component either to enlighten it or perhaps to feature as a climax. Sometimes, having identified the human experience it is better to begin there.

We will take four quite different kinds of literature because what appeals to one is unlikely to appeal to another: a simple story which in this case we will relate to harvest; a Russian novel which will take us to questions of personal relationships; a

musical which will give us insight into a Jewish approach to the
fullness of life; and an incident from an autobiography on what it
means 'to break bread'.

A *harvest parable*

In 'The Bag Lady'[56] we saw the possibility of taking a story and
using it as a basis for the development of ideas rather than as an
illustration, thus enabling the story to speak for itself whilst
sketching in alternative backgrounds so as to bring out the
flavour. Another story which lends itself to this process is 'The
Budgie of St Tropez'.

It concerns a lady who bought a pet budgerigar. This refused to
talk despite all her efforts, so she took it back to the shop and
complained. First, the shopkeeper suggested she might give it a
toy. She did, but it still didn't talk. Next he suggested a mirror.
The result was the same. Third, a playmate, but still not a word
emanated from the budgerigar. Back she went to the pet shop
once more, but this time only to report that the bird had died. 'It's
incredible,' said the shopkeeper; 'in all my experience I have
never known anything like it. Tell me, did the budgerigar never
say a single word?' 'No,' replied the lady, 'not one; except just
before he died, he said, "Food! For goodness sake, give me
food".'

The story is a parable and, like the parables of Jesus, depends
on its setting for its original meaning and on its editors and
raconteurs for subsequent usage.[57]

First, provide a setting (or a variety of settings) which enables
the hearer to identify your budgie. The figure is clearly someone
who depends on you for his livelihood. So, a century ago, if you
were a man of property, it might be your staff or your family. If,
on the other hand, you had no property, it might be the people
you worked for, because in a different way *their* livelihood
depended on *you*. If you are clergy, it might be the parishioners; if
you are a churchgoer, it might be the clergy. You can no doubt
think of others, but in the context of harvest thanksgiving your
'pet budgie' easily becomes the man, the woman and the child in
the Third World. Paint a picture of 'this helpless creature', not as

someone begging for our help (the budgie never even asked to be bought), but as 'a thing of beauty' who asked for so little, yet suddenly found itself in an alien environment. Try a few moments' reflection on why we 'bought our bird' and accepted responsibility for it.

Second, elaborate some of the ways in which he never quite did what we hoped. He didn't 'speak our language'. He never seemed even to grasp what was wanted. Before we took him over, and to some extent even after, he maintained a glowing picture of our way of life, until he travelled for himself and came into our homes only to discover how inaccurate his picture had been. No wonder he remained silent!

Third, explore the methods we have used over the years 'to get him to talk'. The toy. Education? Literacy? The Bible and the hymnbook as tools? The budgie seemed to see through it, as if to say, 'She hasn't given me a toy because she wants me to have a toy. She's given me a toy because she wants me to talk.' The toy was not a love gift; it was simply a means to an end. Then came the mirror. Medicine? The missionary doctor? The budgie saw through that, too. And the playmate. Overseas aid? Projects? Training, treaties and trade? Still not a live bird who would respond as an equal, but rather a dumb animal who had got everything perfect except the capacity to relate. And even then it just might have worked, because apparently at last the bird did actually say something in the right language. But it was too late. What he so desperately needed were the basics. And nobody seemed to have thought of them. Yet he knew the vital word – possibly because that was what the woman herself had said most often when she wasn't actually trying to teach him anything else?

If the story is told simply, some of the judgments will be harsh, and some members of the congregation are likely to be offended. But there is a possibility of a recovery if we are prepared to see that though one generation has died with the budgie's cry on its lips, there are still thousands of others for whom there is time. If the story leads us to see this and change our approach, it will have done its work. Maybe the budgie will only ever speak in its own language, but what is so wrong with that? On the other hand,

116   *Preaching as Theatre*

with a different approach real communication becomes possible in ways never foreseen – we may even learn its language!

Three kisses

Tolstoy's *Resurrection* provides a useful way of exploring the different levels of personal relationship and perhaps telling us something we need to know but would prefer not to hear. The overall story is brief and could be taken almost from the cover blurb, but only by reading the book will you get a feel for what is going on and establish your own points of contact.

Set in the days before the Revolution, it is the story of a Russian Prince, Nekhlyudov, who as a young man seduces a servant girl in the home of his aunts when he is visiting. Years later he sits on the jury at the trial of a prostitute, Katusha, and in the course of the proceedings realizes that it is the same girl. Sensing that he is partly responsible for her plight, and that her sentence is unjust, he sets out to save her from further suffering, humiliation and exile to Siberia by offering to marry her. When she rejects him he decides nevertheless to stay with her, and the story is mainly of his journey to Siberia and his frequently frustrated attempts to get her sentence quashed and to take her as his wife.

In the course of the story Nekhlyudov kisses Katusha three times. First, when he visits his aunts as an innocent young man and the two of them play together in the garden. This is the kiss of innocence – not without feeling but harmless, spontaneous and momentary. Second, when he returns years later, by which time they have both grown older, and he gives her the very formal Russian kiss on both cheeks. Third, when he returns from the roughness of the army and 'life with the boys' for a short visit over Easter, finds her a very attractive girl, kisses her roughly on the neck, pursues her to her bedroom, kisses her rapturously and, in spite of her protests, takes everything else he wants.

Ask how far those three kisses reflect the sad story of all too many human relationships. Kiss number one is the first encounter – innocent interest and genuine attraction. Kiss number two is the formality – custom and tradition. Kiss number three is the kiss of self-satisfaction and exploitation.

Extend the idea at different levels. Marriage, for example. How many marriages – on the suface quite successful marriages over many years – go through the whole gamut, beginning with a genuine mutual attraction, changing into a more formal relationship where there is a job to do, a mortgage to be paid and children to be cared for, but then finishing up where something somewhere has tipped the scales so that in the end one is quietly living off the other? In the beginning each was an heir, inheriting from the other something lacking in themselves. In the end, one who wanted to become an heir (a whole person) had become a slave.

Explore alternative relationships between children and parents (from the thrill of the baby through the mature and more formal relationships of adults to the exploitative nature of old age), between friends and business partners, between two nations or between the First World and the Third World, and ask whether, sadly and all too often, the three kisses do not symbolize what we do to one another, so that whereas the gospel talks about turning slaves into sons (and heirs), we too often find ourselves embroiled in turning heirs into slaves.

Try to work out why Katusha refuses Nekhlyudov 'the fourth kiss' of marriage. Is it because though he knows he has done her wrong, he has no real appreciation of the damage he has done to her as a person,[58] and that she knows better than he does that until this has been faced there can be no real relationship between them?[59] Or is it that Katusha knows only too well what is going on in his mind, and that his desire to marry her is more because he is worried by the guilt that consumes him than because he actually loves her? 'You exploited me once and set me on the road to ruin,' she says; 'you are not going to use me again in order to work off your debt or to assuage your guilt.' Both reasons may then be explored in relation to the concrete situations set up earlier.

But the message of the gospel is that it doesn't have to be like this. Paul says that slaves can be raised to the level of heirs,[60] and other relevant biblical passages worth introducing to the discussion are the woman who kissed the feet of Jesus (a genuine expression of affection), Moses meeting his father-in-law (a formal meeting) and the kiss of Judas (a kiss of exploitation).[61]

Finally, as so often, you need a concrete example of where what you have been talking about actually exists. Jesus is perhaps the most obvious, if not the most convincing, because the hearers already have him in a special category, but there is plenty of evidence of the way in which he cut through rules and red tape in order to establish and maintain enduring and maturing relationships, to lift unnecessary burdens, to set people free and to turn slaves into heirs. And the difference between Nekhlyudov (who is so much like the rest of us) and Jesus (who is so different) is that one is a son who becomes a slave in trying to redeem *himself*, and the other is a Son who becomes a slave to redeem *others*.

In contemporary terms, Mandela's relationship with South Africa may be a light for us all. Here is a man who said yes to the first two kisses and still studiously resists every encouragement to succumb to the third. His own people and his heritage are still important to him, and Anthony Sampson[62] reported recently how he had bought a spacious but unpretentious bungalow not far from where he was brought up so that he can continue to take his holidays there. He also knows the importance of true love and a proper acknowledgment of hurt if a lasting relationship is to be built, especially in a situation where, accordingly to Sampson, efforts to achieve reconciliation are still worryingly one-sided. 'We can neither heal nor build,' he said in his opening speech to Parliament, 'with the victims of past iniquities forgiving and the beneficiaries merely content in gratitude.'

So we are left with a choice. We can turn heirs and sons into slaves, and live with the guilt of it for the rest of our lives. Or we can turn slaves into sons and heirs, and so share in the ministry of Jesus. But if we are tempted to the second, it might be worth pausing if only for a moment to remember what happened to him.

Lohayim! To life!

What are we to understand by eternal life? The life that will never die? The life that is unable to separate us from the love of God? A preacher who is always on the look-out for a new way of presenting the familiar could do worse than use some of the Jewish insights in *Fiddler on the Roof*.

First, in no more than two or three sentences, establish the idea that it has something to do with believing, trusting and looking forward even when everything is against you. The Old Testament is full of it. Sarah's giggle at the news that she is pregnant.[63] Shadrach, Meshach and Abednego's defiance of an arrogant king and a burning fiery furnace.[64] Jeremiah buying a plot of land when the outlook is bleak and the stock market at rock bottom.[65]

But the opening lines of *Fiddler* may be a much more meaningful way into the problem for twentieth-century Britain than a burning fiery furnace. A fiddler perched high up on the roof 'trying to scratch out a simple tune without breaking his neck'.[66] Already some listeners will have identified with him. They will know just how he feels. Others may need a little help, and a few incidents from recent press and television programmes will put flesh on the idea. Describe in *human* terms some of the people who stand behind the unemployment *statistics*, and others in work but with no idea whether they will be in six months' time. Try to get every member of the congregation to see that in one way or another, at some time or other, we are all 'fiddlers' perched on roofs.

Secondly, ask where in 'the fiddler' we can find faith. This may be a little like looking for water in the desert. You won't find it on the surface. You have to prod around. But when you do, you will find the musical rich in material, containing experiences with which we are all familiar and with no shortage of biblical references. A Jew trying to work out why it is that some are rich and some are poor. A father trying to come to terms with changing patterns of marriage and a different attitude in the next generation. A whole village uprooted, dispossessed and persecuted. Parallel contemporary experiences abound to get the congregation feeling rather than thinking.

Ponder the moment when they are all being turned out of their homes and a younger man says to the rabbi, 'Rabbi, we were always taught that in a time of crisis and suffering Messiah would come. Wouldn't it be a good time for him to come right now?' And the rabbi replies, 'Maybe it would . . . but I suspect now we'll have to wait for him some place else.' From there explore the notion of faith in life not as fulfilment but as trust. Not the birth of

Isaac. Not even the coming of the Messiah, but the waiting and the hoping.

Choose your material carefully, but from this point one or two contemporary stories ought to move the emotions steadily on. A nation like Poland, for example, which in spite of all its history went through the darkest days of martial law in the early 1980s convinced that for the faithful it was a day of opportunity. Young people of whom one reads in the press, and especially in the colour supplements, who hang on in spite of everything – always hoping and trusting. This is fiddler faith!

The words of the song 'Lohayim' say it all. Life with all its ups and downs. Life with all its frustrations. Yet the life that is at the centre of it all is the life of God that goes on. This is the life that we celebrate on Easter Day. This is the life that will never die. This is why we are 'more than conquerors',[67] for this life is God.

Other songs and other lines will suggest other themes or further elaborate this one. However, it is not the ideas that matter so much as the feeling, first of identification with the fiddler and then of discovering faith and life as he does. For this purpose a judicious use of the music may be a help.

The breaking of bread

After a reading of the Feeding of the Five Thousand,[68] focus on the difference between breaking the bread and clearing up the crumbs and use whatever method seems appropriate to get people to decide whether they see themselves as 'breakers of bread' or 'crumb-clearers', and which they would prefer to be.

To help the listeners to identify with you, describe one or two of the crumb-clearers you have known and say where you put yourself, but then sharpen the picture by reference to John Osborne who tells in his autobiography[69] how when he was a child he had a girl playmate. He loved her room because there were things everywhere, whereas all the rooms in their house were bare – 'like a doctor's waiting room without the maga-zines!'. He had another playmate – a boy this time – whose mother was 'absently-mindedly welcoming' and in whose home you were just accepted as an extra place-setting, whereas playmates who came to Osborne's home were 'frowned on on arrival and reviled after they had gone'. What mattered was tidying up! Then comes the crunch line:

> If my mother asked you to break bread with her, she was only thinking of how long it would be before she could start clearing up after you.

The two types having been established, perhaps with reference to other contemporary material or characters, try to get the congregation thinking of people they know in these terms. Their favourite politician, actor, church leader, sports person, even their friends. And not only individuals, but perhaps nations, clubs, lobbies or campaigning organizations. What is their prime motive in existing – is it breaking bread or clearing up crumbs?

By this stage people should not only be recognizing the two categories but developing feelings and identifying with one or other. Moreover, since they have no idea where you are going, they are prevented from trying to think and do the right thing. This makes it much more likely for 'something to happen' as you continue.

Look at the world of sport, especially the spirit behind the Olympic Games, and try to imagine life within the Olympic Village. Contrast the joy of the games and the politics that surround them. Is it true that the political people are primarily concerned with tidiness, whereas the sports people can tolerate rough edges? Of course it is not true of *every* politician nor of *every* sports person – but in general?

Or what are we to make in this context of Clean-up TV campaigns or restrictions on the press to protect privacy, etc.? What do the crumb-clearers really *think* they are doing? Do they imagine they can really establish a time when evil will have passed away, when everybody will be nice to everybody else, lions and lambs living together and so on? Or is this just the stuff of poetry? And in a world where everything has to be in its place, like a sheep-dog manoeuvring every animal into position, there is very little left to offer except anger and indignation when it goes wrong, and what are we to do with the people who don't actually fit?

In that last sentence we have suddenly moved on. How different are our hearers' feelings when they realize that now we are not talking about things but about people? So, having touched a nerve, press gently further. Introduce the story of the wheat and the tares. This seems to suggest that breaking bread rather than clearing-up crumbs may be nearer to the gospel. There is room here for God's untidiness.

The final thrust may then be at different levels. What does this say to me about the sort of person I ought to be? About the sort of church I ought to be encouraging? About the sort of society I ought to be creating? Ideally, raise the questions by telling the stories and arousing the feelings.

When Alan Webster was offered the job of Dean of St Paul's by James Callaghan it was reported that he asked Callaghan, 'What do you think is the purpose of the church of God in these days?' After a pause Callaghan is said to have replied, 'To keep people looking outwards'. Not bad, for an off-the-cuff answer.

And not a bad motto for the preacher either.

5

Changing Gear

In the section on 'The prophetic tradition'[1] I said that preachers addressing the prophets today may need to conduct a steady campaign to justify what they are doing. This is not entirely because all change calls for justification and explanation, but because it is often not realized how all preaching is to a large extent the product of its day.

The sermons of the early church fathers, for example, would hardly be acceptable to a congregation today, and nobody would expect them to be. Great preachers like Spurgeon and Wesley would either fail abysmally if they preached their original sermons today, or would have to demonstrate that their true greatness lay not in what they said nor in their interpretation but in their capacity to touch 'the nerve' of their hearers now as then with a totally different kind of product. Preaching is also the product of local culture. One expects an African to preach like an African, a Caribbean like a Caribbean, not like an Englishman or a North American. So it is always worth looking to current trends in any culture to see what is happening and how preaching can be more effective.

Even a cursory glance at the Western world towards the end of the twentieth century suggests that patterns are changing. Sermons tend to be getting shorter. People who are treated to radio and television where the scene is constantly changing are much less disposed to sit still listening to a monologue for more than twenty minutes, however good the preacher is and however much the preacher may protest that 'my people are different and like it', than were their grandfathers, to whom a fifty-minute lecture on anything of educational interest would be judged worth struggling with. This is not so in the Third World or in

parts of Eastern Europe, where long utterances are still acceptable, though how long they will remain so with the advent of
ever-increasing Western radio, video and television is doubtful.

Sermons also have to be interesting. You can no longer assume
that the congregation will struggle with you on the principle that
the more difficult it is to understand what you say, the higher your
intellectual ability. Sermons must be relevant. Congregations
want something that touches their life 'at the sharp end', not
something of purely academic interest. Sermons must begin
where people are, not where the preacher is and thinks they ought
to be. Sermons must be relatively self-contained and self-
explanatory. You cannot assume that everyone has 'seen the
previous episode', so the days of continuity and steady teaching
built up week by week have gone, except in a few rare places. And
sermons must be self-explanatory. Few preachers today would
expect their listeners to be familiar with even a few of the more
common Greek words. Many would not even expect them to be
familiar with Gospel stories, never mind the Old Testament or the
more familiar points of Pauline thinking, so that casual references
and allusions are nearly always out and full details must be in.

If all these points seem obvious, then it can only be because of
the force of change which has taken place. Fifty years ago, they
would not have been anything like so obvious, though even now
there are no doubt more congregations than one imagines who
wish that they could find evidence for them, and perhaps more
preachers than one would wish who would want to contest them.
But for the most part the changes are peripheral. They are not
touching the fundamental emphasis which still sees preaching as
teaching or lecturing, commenting on the scriptures, interpreting
them in relation to life, drawing morals from them, providing
instruction on how to live the Christian life, and then inviting
people either to make fundamental decisions or to go away and
practice what they have heard.

Any 'change of gear', therefore, requires us to look at what it
means to move from preaching as teaching to preaching as event,
noting especially how ingrained and inadequate the 'teaching'
concept is, and how, secondly, the call to see preaching as event is
coming from other places. Thirdly, we need to look at such

changes against the background of other recent trends in biblical and theological study.

Preaching as teaching

As an example of what I mean by 'teaching sermons' I shall take the Mowbray Preaching Series.[2] The range of titles[3] alone makes the point, but if that were not enough the Introduction by the series editor spells it out,[4] when he says that since people need theology but are unlikely to read it, it must therefore be preached, though he admits that it requires considerable adaptation if the resulting sermons are to be palatable for the average congregation.

If we take this as a typical example of preaching in the classical tradition of mainstream Anglicanism and non-conformity in the latter half of the twentieth-century, what is on offer? Here are one or two examples almost at random, beginning with Ford's *Preaching on Great Themes*. Overall the approach is thoroughly biblical, rooted and grounded in everyday life, complete with seminal ideas and appropriate illustrations. The result is a commendable attempt to spoon-feed clergy for the ultimate benefit of their congregations. So far, so good! The objective is unexceptionable and the ideas and presentation are helpful. It is when it comes to the adaptation, method and presentation that questions have to be asked.

First, *the results are unashamedly cerebral*. The preacher is sharing and trading ideas, even giving explanations, but is scarcely ever stimulating thought and is paying scant attention to the emotions. Indeed, these sermons seem almost to belong to the school of thought which would be ashamed to have anything to do with emotions! The whole tenor suggests that preachers expect their hearers to respect their knowledge, understanding and even their opinions, and clearly hope that once they see things their way they will no longer have any problem. The fact that the hearer may have a problem, not with the ideas but with the emotions that accompany the idea, is scarcely entertained, so that at times the ending reads almost like a cry of a despair from one who knows that the hearers are not going to do what they are asked (or told), but 'Oh, if only they would . . .'

For this reason, if we have any communication at all, it is one-way communication. The preacher knows what is on offer, determines the content, and uses the best means available to get it across. The congregation, on the other hand, is a pot waiting to be filled. What is missing is the recognition that every pot is different, that the pot also has needs to be met which are just as real as the goods the preacher has to deliver, and that there may already be something in the pot which will instantly react with what the preacher tries to put there. At best, going to church may be like turning up at the supermarket to find that though it has roughly what you want, the makes are all wrong, and some of the goods are incompatible with the equipment and fittings you already have; at worst it is like turning up at the supermarket to find that the owners that day have turned it into a garden centre.

Of course no preachers can be expected to cater for infinite variety and for every need in every sermon, because (as we have seen) most of this they cannot be expected even to be aware of. However, preachers could at least acknowledge that the need is there and not assume that everything begins and ends with them.

A useful indicator of the way in which preachers see themselves is the way in which they use illustrations. What usually happens is that either they fail to use illustrations at all, or they simply use them to illustrate a point which they want to get across anyway. Sometimes the point is so obvious that no illustration is needed, but the illustration helps to fill out the twenty minutes. Sometimes the story illustrates exactly what the preacher wants to say, but since the preacher has told you beforehand what it is supposed to say to you, the story has effectively been prevented from saying anything else. Again, the impression created is that all that matters is that the preacher's 'brilliant idea' should somehow find its way from their head to your head.

For clarification, compare that with the way in which a novelist tells a story or a dramatist introduces you to plot or character. In both cases they produce a reaction. You like the story or the character or you don't. You see yourself (or somebody else) up there. The writer has no knowledge of this and is content to remain in ignorance. But something is set off in you, and you become a different person as a result of it. Stories, life experiences, newspaper extracts, news items, soaps and all kinds of narratives can all be used in this open-ended way to create a sermon that can have the same effect, but are often not. That way the preacher loses control of what is coming across, and control is what preachers like to think they keep.

Richard Lischer[5] describes many sermon illustrations as 'joins' between religion and the contemporary world, needed because we have already come to the conclusion that the two worlds are far apart and then gone on to assume that the middle ground which links the two is 'the enduring and universal stuff of human experience'. Often illustrations derive their authority not from reflection on the text nor from their appropriateness to the gospel, but from 'the accuracy with which they reproduce our favourite or most fearful experiences'. Thus the sermon becomes little more than 'a vehicle for free-floating inspirational experiences, which are at best tangentially related to a religious truth or a vivid detail in a Bible passage'.

Secondly, *it is not always clear what it is the hearer is expected to do next.* There is talk of the church's ministry as 'preaching for a verdict', 'proclaiming so as to evoke the response of faith', but it is never clear just what sort of verdict is being expected. Endings are not everything, but they are important and, like illustrations, provide a useful clue as to what preachers think they are doing.

So, for example, in a sermon on 'An Active God',[6] the last paragraph appeals to us not to throw away our Bibles with our old newspapers because we need them to strengthen our belief in an active God, when what we really need is something that actually makes us aware of his activity. We need to see and feel something God is actually doing and of which we were totally unaware when we entered church. It may excite us, rouse our curiosity or even make us angry, but if it works, it will send us off on a quest to find God and see what else he is up to. We might then not want to throw away our Bibles because we have suddenly found a new use for them. We might begin to read them in a different way. We might make our own discoveries and tell the preacher next week of ways in which this God is active that even the preacher doesn't know about. All of which would be far better than hoarding Bibles because the preacher says so or arguing in the porch because we think that the preacher hasn't got it quite right. What the original ending does is to leave me unclear as to whether the preacher wants me to believe in an active God or to read my Bible, but on either count it is clearly something this person has in mind that I am to do, not something in me that the preacher is hoping God will set alight as a result of the words of the sermon.

Take another example. In a sermon on 'Evolution with Faith'[7] in a scientific age, in a world in which 'faith has gone out' and 'scepticism is come in', the sermon ends, 'Who is there who does not see the need for the re-establishing of faith in our scientific age? This is why I have preached this difficult sermon.' We will ignore the last sentence,[8] but what am I supposed to do with the question before it? Answer it? Say I do know somebody? Or is it meant to be rhetorical? But whatever it is, what does it actually do for me? Either the sermon has led me to feel this, in which case the sentence is superfluous, or it hasn't. But if it hasn't, that sentence is certainly not going to do it.

Similarly, in a sermon on 'The Bible and Providence',[9] after two or three extraordinary stories, we are left with the question as to whether they are 'mere coincidences' or 'divine providence at work'. It is clear what the preacher believes, and therefore what answer is expected. But how am I supposed to arrive at an answer except by simply agreeing? And what difference will it make whichever answer I give? Could the sermon not at least have done something to make me feel in my bones that what I would always have regarded as pure coincidence might at least have just a little bit of something more going for it? In fairness, this preacher does at least seem to be aware of the problem, but then resorts to the 'ought-type' of ending. In other words, if I believe it is providence, then I *ought* to take the Bible more seriously and be less anxious. If I believe it is pure coincidence then perhaps I *ought* to do something about my faith, though this is not actually said!

Of course the examples may be challenged, but the questions to be asked are: what is it that preachers who preach in this way are trying to do? Which part of the human anatomy are they aiming at? What sort of response would they regard as satisfactory? And what do the hearers imagine that the preachers want? There are many possible answers. Maybe the preachers are trying to get across a new idea: something you didn't know or believe and they want you to grasp it. Maybe a new commitment, like a change of life style or a new year resolution. Maybe solving a puzzle: they want you to go on thinking about something, sorting it out, arguing over the dinner table.

But supposing they wanted to create in you a feeling – a thrill perhaps, or maybe just something less than quiet satisfaction as you leave church. You may not know what it is or why you have it, but it was a twitch somewhere inside. It isn't an answer, and it may not be world-shattering, but working it out in prayer and reflection over a few days could enable the Word of God to come alive in a new way that the preacher never even dreamed of. Then something would have happened. Preaching would have become 'an event'.

Preaching as event

Preaching as event is personal. It is personal to the preacher. No two preachers are going to see or 'paint' the scene in the same way. Truth comes through personality. But preaching is also personal to the hearer. Nobody else in church will see or hear as you do. What happens is inter-action between you and the message. This is a form of preaching that has become more popular in recent years, as one or two recent books on the subject suggest the need for more far-reaching and fundamental changes in our approach, and it is these trends which help to reinforce and develop the sort of things we have been exploring.

Having spent years listening to student sermons and anxious to raise the quality, Richard Lischer,[10] for example, puts his finger on the conflict for many preachers between the exegetical classes in which they are taught to value the text and seek its historical meaning and the pulpit where they find themselves asking, not 'What is the text saying?' but 'What do my people need to hear?', and then try to solve the conflict by resorting to a string of illustrative stories and illustrations 'that often overshadows the matter of the thing to be illustrated'.

Imagination in preaching, he continues, is not

> clever stories or aesthetically-pleasing images . . . It is not even
> discovering elements of analogy between the text and the
> contemporary world in order to make the text relevant. The
> work of the imagination is knowing how to read texts in such a
> way that they will be allowed to function according to their
> original power and intent. The preacher holds the text like a
> precious stone and turns it against the light until its greatest
> brilliance is revealed . . . The genius of preaching lies in the
> discovery of this witness . . . in a moment of theological
> insight.[11]

One consequence of this is that:

> When we talk about preaching 'conveying Christ' we are not
> thinking about talking or explaining, or even hearing, but
> about the sort of preaching that actually makes something
> happen in a person's life.[12]

In a later *Festschrift* contribution, Lischer[13] takes up the idea of
'preaching as event' and argues that what preaching does is to
mediate an experience which has the potential of isolating the
hearer in a private encounter with the word and abstracting the
worshipper from the church, though he has some hesitations
about the idea of personal encounter, because he believes that
part of the answer lies in giving greater attention to the church.

Two other recent books make a similar point, though coming
at it more from the practical than from the theological angle. One
is *Effective Preaching* by Dan Hook, to whom I have already
referred.[14] Hook says that all the good homilies he has heard
have two common characteristics.[15] First, 'each became a vehicle
for an actual experience of God', sometimes passing, sometimes
quite profound. Second, each has in some way or other called him
to change. The important thing about religious experiences for
Hook[16] is that 'they tend to "break in" upon us' and are a
mixture of the finite human situation and the 'mystery' of God.
They are a gift inviting response, and though preachers may
contribute to them, they can never actually initiate them. All they
can do is 'dispose' people to experience God.

The reason why much traditional Western preaching fails to do this, Hook believes,[17] is that it is too conceptual and too preoccupied with ideas. This he attributes to the mind-set dominated by the English language, which is heavily grammatical and conceptual, good on definition and description but sadly lacking when it comes to things visual, and not at its best when it comes to imagination. Yet this is the language of education and therefore the language in which theology is taught. Students therefore become

> capable of discussing theological principles and perspectives, but rarely develop the skills of being able to theologize in a pastoral setting. Theology, rather than theologizing, is taught.

The result is that preachers spend hours clarifying and defining the ideas they wish to communicate, after which their sole purpose is to convince their hearers of their validity. To this extent Hook is describing precisely what I was illustrating earlier.[18] He acknowledges that hearers like this approach, that it can be effective, and that it has made a substantial contribution to the life of the community over the centuries and will continue to do so. The trouble is that too many preachers have become slaves to it. 'They neither knew, nor felt the need to know, any other style,' whereas preaching 'involves much more than the communication of ideas. It is about experience of God and conversion.'[19]

The other book is *Preaching as Weeping, Confession, and Resistance. Radical Responses to Evil* by Christine Smith. The sub-title is 'Radical Responses to Radical Evil', and in this context radical evil is handicapism, ageism, heterosexism, sexism, white racism and classism. Preaching, for Smith, is a craft in which three worlds converge: the world of the text, the world of the preacher and community where proclamation occurs, and the world of the larger social context in which we live our lives of faith. 'Often in homiletics,' she writes, 'there is a primary emphasis on the world of the text', whereas in this book she wants to reflect on the wider social context in which we live our lives of faith.[20] It is not a book of sermons – more a collection of raw material for sermons, perhaps! But the author certainly doesn't want preachers to conceptualize on these issues. Instead she wants them first to learn how to share these human experiences in depth (that is weeping), then to 'name' or spell out precisely what it is that is evil (that is confession), and finally to use the act of preaching itself to initiate actual moves to resistance. In three sermons of her own which she appends to the text she then gives some examples of how she herself has tried to do this.

What these books have in common is that they all refer to or require a much greater use of the imagination than has normally been permissible (let alone encouraged) in much Western theological education. But imagination in preaching, according to Paul Scott Wilson,[21] does not mean one particular form of preaching, such as narrative, though it is often so interpreted, and is more than creativity. It is a way of thinking that contrasts with logic and yet is complementary to it. Indeed imagination and logic are two ways of thinking or two qualities of thought: whereas logic is 'primarily unidirectional or linear, moving step-by-step to a specific purpose or intent', imagination 'finds a meaningful connection between two dissimilar ideas that have no causal relationship'.

Having clarified what he means by imagination, Wilson then focusses on three areas where imagination is vital for excellent preaching: interpretation of the Bible, discernment of God's action in the world, and presentation of the mystery of God (past, present and future). Imagination in biblical interpretation certainly does not mean reading into the text things which are not there, but it does mean reading more carefully and critically, and with an open mind. It means learning to recognize the over-riding 'concerns' of a text and coming to terms with the fact that every text may have more than one meaning.

Wilson's comments on the 'concerns' of the text also help us to handle the problem of a double hermeneutic to which I referred several times. The concerns of the text, he says,[22] are located in the past. What the preacher has to do is to put the same idea in the present tense; it may then become the concern of the sermon.[23] Already then there is a spark between the two concerns. This is a process which is unconscious every time we preach. Then comes the main point,

By making it conscious, we identify theme statements for individual paragraphs (or groups of paragraphs) in *a sermon that moves, possibly several times, into the text and then back to our situation* (italics mine).

From there Wilson goes on to set out some homiletical strategies for incorporating these ideas into preaching. However, this 'movement' that 'sparks concerns' is the subject of the book, as many of the examples will have testified.

Perhaps the last word in this section should go to Walter Brueggemann, who says that each one of us has 'a zone of imagination that stands between the input of the text and the outcome of attitude, belief or behaviour'.[24] It is partly shaped by the community to which we belong, but is also a very personal zone ('a protected place of intimacy and interiority that I keep for my very self'), and therefore nobody ever knows what is really going on there. What the preacher needs to remember, however, is that in the moment of hearing this place is not empty and unoccupied. 'It is a busy, teeming place with the hearer's own powerful vested interests, deep fears and old unresolved hurts.' It is into this zone of imagination that preachers might profitably tap more usefully and more often, whilst always remembering that they cannot control what will happen there, neither can they be held responsible for the consequences.

Trends in biblical and theological study

Increasing openness to a variety of interpretations of preaching and sermons also chimes in with changing trends in other places, as biblical scholars and theologians learn to relate to each other's craft and so come to recognize varieties of interpretation which would have been unthinkable half a century ago.

Some evidence for this is provided by James D. G. Dunn and James P. Mackey in their Editors' Foreword to the SPCK series, Biblical Foundations in Theology. 'The aim of this series,' they write, 'is to bridge the gap between biblical scholarship and the larger enterprise of Christian theology', because though biblical scholars see themselves as contributing to theology, and theologians regard the Bible as their ultimate court of appeal, 'yet the gap remains', and too often theologians have forced a meaning on a text 'which they could have better understood' while biblical scholars have produced theologies which often owed too much 'to prevailing theological fashions'. Hence a series of books written by two authors, one from each discipline.

Further evidence may be found in the fact that a conference on Bible and Theology organized by King's College, London, in March 1995 attracted some eighty biblical scholars and theologians.[25] The conference was important not so much for what it achieved as for what it marked. Such a conference had not happened before, and probably even a decade ago would not have been thought of. Its principal architect was Francis Watson, whose own commitment to bridging the gap between biblical scholarship and systematic theology is well known, and whose recent book[26] bears witness to it. His concern to bring together text, church and world and his insistence that Bible reading is an enterprise in 'seeking to discern the truth' has particular relevance for preachers, as does his recognition of the impact of narrative theology and feminist theology on biblical hermeneutics.

To this may be added a recent collection of essays[27] by distinguished theologians and biblical scholars as well as preachers showing an immense variety of ways in which preachers use the Bible. The revised edition (1993) found it necessary to add some interpretations not included at all in the original (1985).[28] The book is also more than theory, in that after an exposition of the way in which each tradition handles scripture in preaching, there is a sermon by someone of distinction within that tradition which is useful not simply for its breadth but also for the way in which it demonstrates that there is never only one meaning to be discovered or one interpretation to be accepted.

All these trends have consequences for the preacher.

First, *they reinforce the manifold ways of interpreting a sermon by demonstrating that there is always more than one way of interpreting a biblical passage.* There always has been, of course,[29] as anyone who reads some of the early church interpretations or the writings of the seventeenth-century Reformers will testify, but just as there is a tendency for the nonspecialist who has been told the meaning of a Bible story in his youth to spend the rest of his life unquestioningly believing that that is all it means, so also there is a danger that preachers may take the biblical and theological scholarship of the last fifty years as the last word said (during their years of training!) and refuse to appreciate that 'the Lord has yet more light and truth to break forth from his Word'. The bringing together of biblical and theological scholarship may result in a creativity that goes some way to correct this perspective and do much to discourage the notion that what the preacher says is not only 'how it is for *the preacher* on that particular morning' but also how it ought to be for everybody who is listening. It just isn't! Worshippers have their own agenda when they arrive. They have their own interpretation and therefore their own agenda when they depart. Good preaching must allow for this and not regard it as a failure 'to get it across'.

Second, *the realization that the search for the truth calls for the need to involve more than one group in the hermeneutical process*. Francis Watson's plea[30] that 'seeking to discern the truth' calls for 'text, church and world' to be involved together must not go unheeded, because if any of those three parties is missing, the truth will be stunted, and because it is only by bringing those three parties together that we can be saved from any number of limited and partisan interpretations. The preacher must therefore clearly allow for this in preaching, and those outside the church as well as the congregations must assist in the interpretative process. But then the people in the pew also must make room for it, and allow the interpretations they arrive at to be put to the same test.

Such methods also open up the possibility that when scripture is interpreted in these ways 'something happens'. People are not being taught or told what to believe. They are engaging in a process – you could say that they are engaging with God. Of course they won't always hear clearly what God says; they will misunderstand and they will be biassed according to their experiences and all that has gone before. But they will not be more so than any preacher, and at least they will be making the discovery and experiencing it for themselves, not clogging their mind with other people's misconceptions or their heart with guilt because they cannot either understand or do everything that is being put in front of them.

Third, current trends *reinforce the idea that interpretations differ according to who is doing the interpreting.* Restrict it to the men, the rich, or the professionals and it will fall out one way. Let in the women and the poor and don't be surprised if they see it differently. Hence the impact of the arrival of feminist theologies, sociological readings, narrative theology, Third World theologies, liberation theology, and so on.

In a paper given to the Society for Old Testament Sudy,[31] for example, David Clines suggested that the Ten Commandments very much reflect middle-class, male, conservative values of the day.[32] The people who want to prevent stealing are those who have something to steal. The people who want to prohibit work on the Sabbath are those who are engaged in occupations which can stop for the Sabbath and in which they can earn enough money to live by working only on six days. On the other hand, there is very little that seeks to protect the rights of those who are dispossessed. And so on. Whether you agree with Clines or whether he proves his case is beside the point. What is undeniable is that once someone has sown this thought in your mind, it is difficult ever to see the Ten Commandments in the same way again. A rich, middle-class, conservative man will certainly want to argue with Clines. A poor, working-class, radical woman may feel she knew it all along. In both cases something has happened.

Fourth, the new trends demonstrate that *interpretations differ according to where you do them.* As long as the Catholics or the Pentecostals can keep the discussions to themselves, the answers will fall out one way. Involve the Reformed or the Orthodox and the answers will come out differently. Restrict them to the plusher parts of Europe and North America and they will reflect European and North American culture. Let them loose in the *favelas* of Brazil or almost any other part of South America, and they will reflect something different. The result may be described as contextual hermeneutics. The Third World provides a good example of the way in which they work.

Third World interpretations

There are many ways in which Third World theology is making its impact. Liberation theology is only one of them. *Voices from the Margin* is a volume of essays by Third World scholars expanding on the insights of Latin American liberation theology and going on to develop their own interpretative styles and strategies.[33] The 'margin' refers not only to the struggles and exegetical concerns of those who are on the fringe of society, thus introducing issues and topics not normally found in biblical commentaries and theological textbooks (or, for that matter, in sermons!), but also to the way in which black and other biblical scholars have been marginalized by the predominance of male Euro-American scholarship. This book seeks to redress the balance by bringing together those who have had formal exegetical training and those who have not,[34] which is what the preacher is required to do Sunday by Sunday. 'Third World' in this context, therefore, means all the people who have been excluded from power, 'from the authority to mould and shape their own future – racial minorities, the poor, women, and the marginalized peoples of the world'.[35] It no longer has merely a geographical connotation, nor is it simply a third political force; it is a description of people who face harassment and exploitation wherever they are. What it has to offer, therefore, is a variety of viewpoints well outside the norm or the traditional.[36]

The very existence of the book is ample testimony to the way in which something happens when those in the pew are allowed to read and think for themselves in company with fellow Christians who are facing the same issues and with a preacher who is prepared to listen before speaking and to share with listeners in the interpretative process.[37] To read it is to discover new interpretations of the text and to underline the variety of interpretations that are possible. To study it will provide preachers with tools which they might use in their own situation and a style of preaching which might enable something to happen there.

Sociological and political readings

Similar things have been happening in the world of sociological and political readings of the Bible. A collection of essays first published in 1975,[38] re-issued in an expanded form in 1976[39] and then (in response to demand) revised and expanded in 1983,[40] aimed at bringing to light the social struggles of the biblical communities and the resources they drew on, and then using those struggles to help us in the social struggles we are facing today. Here again, it is helpful to see Hosea as Bible study for Marxist Christians; the alternative approach to biblical texts as a result of a materialist reading of the Bible; recent Marxist readings of the Bible in relation to Jacob and Jesus; and a summary of the reading of the Bible in Latin American liberation theology.

But the major contribution for our purposes is not so much the content of these newer readers as the underlying chasms in biblical interpretation which they bring to light: like the yawning gap between religion and the rest of life, between the past as 'dead history' and the present as 'real life', between thought and practice, and between biblical academics and popular lay study. The case for bridge-building can never have been stronger, and the issues are again the sort of issues that the preacher today is called upon to address.

As for liberation theology, Christopher Rowland and Mark Corner offer a sample of the kind of biblical interpretation now becoming commonplace in Latin America,[41] including both the materialist exegesis which looks at the socio-political dimension of the text in its original context and the readings in the basic Christian communities which relate the biblical stories and images to contemporary struggles for justice.[42] They then proceed to explore the impact of these interpretations on the dominant method of reading the Bible in the North American and European churches and academies, as demonstrated by the work of Carlos Mesters, writing from the perspective of one whose work has involved him in interpreting the Bible with the poor of Brazil.[43]

Feminist readings

Similar things have been happening among women. Feminist theology takes many forms, but one potent form is what happens when a woman is able to combine her woman's eye with biblical scholarship and so see something which male scholarship over the years has missed. Phyllis Trible is a good example. The theory is in *God and the Rhetoric of Sexuality*, in which she pleads for a fresh way of listening to the text so that it can have its own say without excessive manipulation. There is nothing particularly feminine in this. The practice comes through in *Texts of Terror*,[44] a literary study of four biblical stories,[45] each of which has its own poignancy as she re-tells it and forces us to notice what we had always missed. Men and women may respond differently to the interpretation, but it is doubtful if either can ignore it, and once seen it is difficult to forget. Something happens here, too.[46]

Within the varieties of alternative interpretations to which we are now treated it is not always easy or desirable to draw lines of demarcation, and much of Trible's work is as much a literary reading as a feminist one. This naturally leads us to literary readings and narrative theology, taking the texts of the Bible as they have come down to us and treating them as stories.

Narrative theology

Narrative theology (or narrative criticism, as it is sometimes called) is a development of the last twenty to thirty years in Europe and North America, based on the view that whatever else the Bible is, it is first and foremost a collection of literature containing stories. Modern biblical scholarship, with its emphasis on the academic, the historical and the philological, still has its place, but should not be allowed to deflect attention from the literary power and subtlety of the biblical books.[47] Such an emphasis has given rise to a new discipline, practised both by scholars and by straightforward readers who believe that in the Bible they have the text as God intended them to have it and therefore wish to read it for what it is, namely, narrative.[48] To those who are concerned about the truth in the Bible they would argue that there the ancient writers steadily sought to realize through the medium of literature an order of truth that transcends literature.[49]

Unlike liberation and feminist readings, which take their interpretations from the standpoint of the reader, narrative criticism bears some resemblance to the historical-critical method, but derives a different meaning as a result of introducing tools that come from a different discipline. From the preacher's point of view this may create some difficulties, because literary criticism focuses on whole books, whereas the preacher is often expected to focus on one particular story or passage.[50] On the other hand, some of the literary-critical tools can be of special value to the preacher, who may practise applying them in a different way.

It is not my purpose to outline all aspects of literary criticism, but one tool worth mentioning is allusion. This is important because it illustrates well the way in which the allusion may bring new meaning to a text, and also the way in which a preacher may spark off something within the congregation. Alter devotes a whole chapter to showing[51] how allusion is pervasive in the Bible and adds illustrations to show its significance. Once connections are made in the mind of the hearer, a new chain of interpretation is set off. One story speaks to the other, and both may be enriched. Alter goes on in the same chapter to unearth some of the treasures which are new and would probably not have come to light in any other way. The method is new compared to more familiar tools of the historical-critical method, but it is not fundamentally different from the archaeologist bringing new light to the scriptures by digging up Palestine.

The preacher may use allusion in two ways. One, like Alter by enabling scripture to interpret itself in the light of scripture, and two, by choosing words with such care and precision as to stir other ideas and emotions within the congregation so that, like the Jews in Old Testament times, they may spot meanings and hear ideas which enable them to make connections between what the scriptures put before them and the world in which they are living. Such allusions may not convey the force of the preacher whose main concern is to get across ideas and who will use any illustration to achieve it; the method may also be much less reliable as a tool of communication, but it may well prove much more powerful once the connections are made, and much more reliable than anything we are asked to believe because somebody said so.

If 'pulpit', then, is to become 'theatre', a cauldron where things can happen, these are helpful pointers to some of the trends we might follow through in our preaching. Already, no doubt, you, the reader, will have quarrelled with some of my examples. No matter. What is more important is that you use what I have offered to clarify the idea and then find sufficient stimulus to go off in your own direction and make discoveries for yourself.

Additional Note on Sources and Settings

Because this is a book about preaching as theatre and not about homiletics, I have felt no overwhelming urge to get involved in method, which could easily be the subject for another title. There are, however, three points which are so basic to this approach that it would be negligent not to address them.

Sources

Sermons begin in many places. In some traditions they begin with the lectionary. The readings are set out – Old Testament, Epistle and Gospel – and the preacher's job is to relate them, separately or together, to the life of the congregation. In other traditions they begin with the preacher. Faithful preachers read their Bible, say their prayers, search their heart, and by Friday are listening to see what God would have them say. Or, to put it differently, they keep looking for something to say all week and by Friday know they have to say something. Once they know what they want to say, they then look around for a text or a Bible passage and try to work it out with illustrations, anecdotes and application. To some, in all traditions, a sermon begins with an idea. The preacher sees something, hears something, reads something, feels something. This sets the preacher off, just as when Amos saw a basket of fruit (*qayits*) it reminded him of the end (*qets*), and next Sunday's utterance is on its way.

Each starting-place has its strength and weakness. Preaching from the lectionary is often regarded as the safest starting-point. If the lectionary is good and balanced, then overall the preaching is likely to be balanced.[1] It gives preachers a starting-point, and so saves them thrashing around for something every week, and if the congregation is devoted enough to be following the lectionary

themselves, they can adequately prepare for what they may
expect to receive. If the utterance seems to be pointed or ill-
chosen, at least a preacher cannot so easily be accused of getting
across what he or she wants to say under the pretext of
expounding the word. But this approach is not without its
dangers. The fact that there are three readings means that the
method is not without some degree of flexibility; the task of tying
them together is by no means easy, at times almost impossible,
and extremely difficult if the end product has to be no more than
ten to twelve minutes in length and anything meaningful is to be
said at all. Furthermore, the readings are not always easy to relate
to the circumstances of the day or the issues that are in the minds
of the congregation, and in the last resort can be every bit as much
a chain as a lead.

However, preachers who eschew the readings, on the grounds
that they must 'preach from the heart' (as if that were the
alternative), know that their method, too, has its pitfalls. It is far
too easy to have a limited range of topics and an even more
limited range of Bible readings, not to mention hymns, and there
are times when limited lines can become very threadbare, as many
congregations can testify. Such preachers know the danger of
being criticized for preaching their own ideas rather than
expounding the Word, and at times using their pulpit as a
coward's castle. They know, too, the struggle that goes with
trying to find something fresh, or dressing up familiar ideas in
new clothes. It is true that their freedom does enable them to
address the scriptures week by week, to read the newspaper and
watch the television, to visit their congregation and pray for their
needs, and then on Sunday to bring it all together in a way that is
liable to be related to that situation and no other. However, it is a
rare skill that can provide this service on a weekly basis; a limited
number of preachers are blessed with it; and training in
theological colleges is not always as helpful as it might be.

Each approach can be used as an excuse for not making any
changes. To both approaches, three things have to be said. First,
they are not mutually exclusive. The lectionary does not preclude
the preacher from using good ideas or personal experiences as
they come along, and the preacher who begins there need not find

it all that restricting. Second, no preacher needs to feel that he or she has to make the ultimate choice. On some occasions there is room for pure lectionary teaching and on others for a gripping idea, though better still might be a combination of the two, allowing each to speak to the other. Change and variety will be healthy for the preacher as for the congregation, and much better than being stuck for ever in one particular rut. But thirdly, and most important, if we are talking about method and presentation so as to allow something to happen, the starting-point matters little. What matters more is what we think we are about and where we go with it.

Some of the examples at which we have been looking would not have been created at all without some unusual personal experience or moment of insight. Others would not have happened if the lectionary had not dictated the line of thought. What is needed is not an either-or but a readiness to adapt to the situation in which we find ourselves, whether it be immediately liberating or confining.

The other point (obvious, but often overlooked) is that the finished sermon need not always begin where the idea began. The lectionary may determine the starting point, but the preacher doesn't necessarily have to begin there in the pulpit. Just as we may major on any of the three readings, and so begin with the one we choose, so also we may begin somewhere else altogether and work back to the readings. The same thing may happen with a blinding insight or a personal experience which gets us going. It may be much more powerful to begin somewhere else and then introduce the insight at the appropriate point. Sometimes, in fact, the insight comes best at the end. Preparing a sermon can be just as much a matter of writing up an introduction to the lessons or the idea and then letting them speak for themselves as writing down a development of them. The crucial question to be addressed is, 'What is this sermon intended to do?' There is no better way of handling that than writing the answer to the question in not more than twenty-five words, and until it is answered there is no way of preparing the sermon effectively.

From this point the danger is that preachers who do this will be accused of manipulation. If they are trying to make something happen, is that not plain manipulation and therefore just as dangerous as trying to get across an idea, if not more so? Yes and no. If preachers are trying to create a certain atmosphere, develop particular attitudes or induce certain emotions, and if they use all the means at their disposal to do so, then yes. Indeed, preachers who behave like that are probably more dangerous than those who are at least content to give people an idea and let them think about it. Shades of the advertising industry, PR and media hype! But if on the other hand the preacher is using all the available resources to present one way of looking at a problem, an issue or an idea and then leaving the hearers with a choice, no. Provided the choice is wide enough. It must certainly be wider than the old evangelical choice of 'accept or reject'. But what is needed is not so much a wider choice as a different kind of choice, perhaps not so much one choice as several choices.

It is rather like painting-by-numbers. True artists can be left to paint on their own. Many of us need help if we are to paint at all, but we don't all need the same kind of help. Some of us need help to draw flowers before we can even begin to think about painting; some need help with colouring the flowers which they can draw perfectly well (if we are not to have red daffodils), and some who can do both still need help with light and shade, balance and everything that goes with that. What none of us wants is a painting-by-numbers book where the whole thing is set out for us in one form so that we all finish up with the same picture, or to be told simply that we can take it or leave it. We would prefer a variety, but again not the variety which says 'This week you can take or leave this', and 'Next week you can take or leave that'. What we want is a varied offering in front of us, so that we can respond in a way which for us is appropriate at that point in our experience. Of course it may not produce the pretty paintings that our preacher/teacher would like us to produce under their tutelage. That would be 'painting for the teacher'. It might mean that some weeks we produce very little at all, and other weeks we go away feeling greatly enriched, though still not necessarily in the way they might have expected or chosen.

The choice, therefore, which the sermon must offer us is, first, between feeling we have to follow the preacher and feeling free to go off on our own – 'to buy the painting' or to paint our own. But if the sermon is going to allow me, indeed stimulate me, to go off on my own, then it has to be open not only at the end but also at the beginning and throughout. At the very beginning I must be offered not only a choice of how I paint but of whether I paint at all, and if I do, what I choose to paint; and at each point I must be offered not only flowers and colours but other possibilities as well. In other words, preachers must know where they are going and what they are hoping to achieve in their congregation (their twenty-five words), but they must then be prepared to work in such an open way that, far from being manipulated, their hearers find an infinite number of possibilities according to where they are and what they need.

And that openness must go back even before the sermon to the service, which must provide a setting.

Settings

The idea of providing a setting is much more likely to appeal to the Free Church preachers than to Anglicans or (possibly) Roman Catholics, if only because Anglicans and Catholics do not normally expect to have to construct the service. They may choose hymns, but they are more likely to be thinking of the place of the hymn in the liturgy (praise, confession, etc.) or of the day in the liturgical calendar than the overall theme of the sermon. Readings are normally stipulated, and so too are most of the prayers, though there is more freedom and variety than there used to be. Free Church preachers, on the other hand, are much more . likely to plan the service as a whole, rather than accept it as a liturgy to which a sermon may be appended.[2]

For maximum impact, however, it is important that the sermon is seen as part of the whole, and for this reason more thought needs to be given not simply to the 'utterance' but to the setting in which it is placed. Hymns and readings, for example, may be chosen to bolster the thrust of the sermon, to contrast with the thrust of the sermon, or to provide balance for the thrust of the sermon, and readings may well be secular and contemporary as well as biblical. In other words, the overall pattern of worship including the sermon is part of the drama.

To this view it is sometimes objected that such an approach is too restricting, and that one needs to preserve the 'objectivity' of the worship, thus leaving the more direct approach for the sermon, but such a response fails to take account of the fact that each act of worship provides a setting anyway. Preachers may think that the act is objective and impersonal until they get to the sermon, but every worshipper knows better. Worshippers are being affected in all manner of ways by what is going on from the moment they enter the building, not least by the emotive power of the music. Failure to appreciate this means that at best the Word sits uncomfortably with the worship and at worst may be nullified by it, so that the issue is not whether or not we provide a setting but whether the one that is there is supportive, merely congenial, hostile or plain indifferent.

Thought therefore needs to be given to the internal appearance and 'decoration' (or impact) of the building as one enters. Posters, notices, pictures, icons, flowers are all part of the scene. Music and readings come next, and the proportionate amount of time for each part of the service third. There is no reason why *every* Sunday the worship should be twice as long as the sermon or vice versa! Variety requires thought from those who lead worship if it is to stimulate thought and feelings in those who participate. Let the plan reflect what one is trying to convey.

Sermons traditionally begin with a text, but it is usually more helpful if the whole act of worship can begin with a theme. Worshippers need signposts from the moment they enter church if they are not to embark on a mystery tour which, exciting or disappointing, may well leave them saying, 'If only I had known where I was going and what to expect I would have appreciated it so much more.' An awareness of the theme, on the other hand, enables the worshipper to reflect imaginatively on the readings and hymns. This is so much more profitable than sitting in silence or engaging in an endless round of chatter, exchanging personal news which can easily wait until afterwards. Nor does it matter if the congregation's thoughts and emotions begin to move in a direction different from what the preacher has in mind. That is all part of the rich tapestry, and any scene and setting in a worshipper's psyche is better than none at all.

Early in the service, a prologue or comment then provides a good opportunity for the preacher to clarify the theme, and if it can be done at a level that will say something to young people, so much the better. They may not grasp all that is involved. They may only remember the story, if that determines the theme, as will some adults, but it is good if the theme can be stated very simply in narrative form in not more than two or three minutes so that whatever happens later, at least each worshipper has got that. The condensation, simplification or explication of the preacher's theme in this way will also be good self-discipline in preparation, and may take as much time and more effort than the later oration. The sermon can then develop this idea either at greater depth (for those who want to probe deeper into ideas or emotions) or at different levels (for those who wish to apply its thrust in different ways, in different places or to different groups).

Once the sermon is over, final prayers may complete the scene, either by continuing the same theme with a different medium, so enabling the worshippers to work out and reflect upon what is happening to them, or by the introduction of complementary ideas and feelings as a recognition that no theme is complete in itself and that some worshippers will have felt that what they have been given is inadequate in isolation.

Matters of technique

Every preacher knows that it is not difficult to hold the attention of children if you have a good story and tell it well, but that they all switch off as soon as you begin to point the moral. (Sadly, too many seem incapable of doing very much about it!) Fewer preachers seem to be aware that they can actually ruin a good sermon by the way they begin. Fewer still have any understanding of the length of time a child can concentrate, particularly if the story-teller is not getting on with it, using two or three times as many words as are needed, or is ir-ritatingly repetitive. Adults are no different. They too have a built-in capacity to switch off as soon as they realize that the preacher is 'getting at them', and are put off by the same signs of a lack of professionalism.

So what might we all learn from a look over our shoulder at broadcasters, writers and dramatists when it comes to brevity, conciseness, capturing human interest and letting our material speak for itself? Since there is no shortage of information and expertise on these topics from which all preachers could benefit, my purpose is not to answer the question but to focus attention on one or two issues and plead that more attention be given to them.

In broadcasting, and particularly in interviewing, there are always two questions to be addressed once everything else has been prepared: how are you going to get in and how are you going to get out? The beginning – because if you lose your listeners there, or get them going in the wrong direction, you may lose them for good; and the ending – because you always have to stop at a given time, and since your 'punch line' is crucial, you must be in the right place at the right time to deliver it. No question of 'rabbitting-on' or running round in circles until you find it! No less attention to these two points is required if a preacher wishes to be effective.

Too many potentially good sermons never stand a chance because the beginning is wasted. A theatre beginning is crisp and intriguing, so either the curtain goes up or the theatre is plunged into darkness and then the light determines what we see. One cannot imagine a play beginning with an actor or a writer giving a long spiel on how he came to write it, why he chose that subject or what happened to him on the way to the theatre. Yet preachers often waste their asset in that way. If things have to be said (and they rarely do if the sermon is properly constructed), they should either be part of the drama (or sermon) itself, be put on a handout, or be said before that point of the service. The beginning is sacred – it is part of 'the plot'.

Much the same is true of endings. Too many 'finallys' may be a killer, but so too is an attempt to sum up. A play may end with a bang or a whimper, and there is nothing wrong in an audience which can see it coming, but they certainly ought not to be able to write the final line. And if it can come in such a way as to surprise them, or leave them with their heart missing a beat, and a feeling that at least they were not prepared for that, so much the better.

A third point is brevity and conciseness. In broadcasting, length and tightness are of the essence. The test is not how short you can make it (the length is usually pre-determined anyway), but how much you can actually say in the time available. Many first-time broadcasters are surprised, not at how little they can say in three minutes, but at how much. Two questions need to be asked of every script: how many words can I do without, and which ideas are extraneous and would have been better not introduced at all? So there are two other questions for a final check: how much actually detracts from what I am trying to achieve, and can anything be excised without the overall thrust being lost?

In preaching, it is a pity that brevity is usually discussed in terms of how long a sermon should be. Conciseness seems not to be addressed at all (thanks to the tolerance of congregations!). Suggestions that we live at a time when concentration is limited, or that we are now 'programmed' to listen only for the three-minute slot or the sound-byte, are not very helpful. They simply put preachers on the defensive with arguments about 'how long my people are prepared to listen'. The issue is not how long it takes, but whether it need take as long as it does. How long do people really need to listen to grasp what we are saying? In some cases five minutes would do it. The rest is padding. In other cases, it may take half an hour, but if it does, might it not be better tackled differently? In two halves, maybe, or with two voices, or even from different places in the church?

Two final points, and since they have run through most of what I have said in the previous chapters I need mention them only for emphasis. First, broadcasters and writers all know the value of the human interest story. Listeners can identify with it in a way they can never identify with ideas and doctrines. Second, it is important to cultivate the skill of letting the material speak for itself. If it is well formulated, it will slip into place without anyone noticing what is happening; if it has to be hammered in, there is something wrong with it.

Bibliography

Books

Alfaro, Juan I., *Micah: Justice and Loyalty*, Handsell Press and Eerdmans, Grand Rapids 1989

Alter, Robert, *The World of Biblical Literature*, SPCK 1992

Alter, Robert and Frank Kermode (eds.), *The Literary Guide to the Bible*, Collins 1987

Anderson, Bernhard W., *The Living World of the Old Testament*, Longmans 1958

Anderson, David, *The Tragic Protest*, SCM Press 1969

Avila, Charles R., *Peasant Theology. Reflections by the Filipino Peasants on their Process of Social Revolution*, WSCF Asia Book 1, Bangkok, c.1975

Barrington, John, *Red Sky at Night*, Michael Joseph 1984

Baxter, Kay, *Speak What We Feel*, SCM Press 1964

Bennett, Arnold, *Anna of the Five Towns*, Methuen 1902 and Penguin 1936

Bethge, Eberhard, *Dietrich Bonhoeffer. Theologian, Christian, Contemporary*, Collins 1970

Bethge, Eberhard, Renate Bethge and Christian Gemmels (eds.), *Dietrich Bonhoeffer. A Life in Pictures*, SCM Press 1986

Bigger, Stephen, *Creating the Old Testament. The Emergence of the Hebrew Bible*, Blackwell 1989

Brenner, A. *The Song of Songs*, Sheffield Academic Press 1989

Brueggemann, Walter, *The Bible and Postmodern Imagination*, SCM Press 1993

Bock, Jerry, Joseph Stein and Sheldon Harnick, *Fiddler on the Roof*, Carlin Music 1974

Ceresko, Anthony R., *Introduction to the Old Testament. A Liberation Perspective*, Orbis Books, Maryknoll, and Geoffrey Chapman 1992

Chekov, Anton, 'The Seagull', in *Chekov Plays* (Penguin Classics), translated by Elisaveta Fen, Penguin Books 1970

Christo, Carlos, *Letters from the Prisoner of Conscience*, Lutterworth 1977

Cox, Harvey, *The Feast of Fools*, Harvard University Press 1969

Davies, Graham I., *Hosea,* Sheffield Academic Press 1993

Davies, J. G., *Every Day God,* SCM Press 1973

Dennis, Trevor, *Lo and Behold! The Power of Old Testament Storytelling,* SPCK 1991

——, *Speaking of God. A Collection of Stories,* SPCK 1992

Donders, Joseph G., 'The Cross: Horizontal and Vertical', in *Jesus the Stranger,* Orbis Books, Maryknoll, 1978, pp. 172–6

Dorfman, Ariel, *Death and the Maiden,* Nick Hern Books 1992

Dudzus, Otto, *Bonhoeffer for a New Generation,* SCM Press 1985

Eliot, T. S., 'The Naming of Cats' (*Old Possum's Book of Practical Cats*), in *Complete Poems and Plays,* Faber and Faber 1969, p. 209

Ford, D. W. Cleverley, *Preaching on Great Themes,* Mowbray 1989

——, *Preaching on the Holy Spirit,* Mowbray 1990

Franck, Frederick, *The Zen of Seeing. Seeing/Drawing as Meditation,* London 1973

Gilmore, Alec, *Tomorrow's Pulpit,* Lutterworth Press and Judson Press 1975

Gottwald, Norman K. (ed.), *The Bible and Liberation. Political and Social Hermeneutics,* Orbis Books 1984

Greene, Barbara and Victor Gollancz, *God of a Hundred Names: Prayers of Many Peoples and Creeds,* Gollancz 1962

Gunn, David M. and Danna Nolan Fewell, *Narrative in the Hebrew Bible,* OUP 1993

Hastings, James (ed.), *Dictionary of the Bible,* T. & T. Clark 1963

Hook, Dan, *Effective Preaching,* E. J. Dwyer 1991

Howatch, Susan, *Absolute Truths,* Harper Collins 1995

Kafka, Franz, *Stories 1904–1924,* a new translation by J. A. Underwood, Futura Macdonald 1983

——, 'The Trial', in *The Complete Novels,* Minerva 1992

Kreitzer, Larry J., *The Old Testament in Fiction and Film,* Sheffield Academic Press 1994

Küng, Hans, *Credo,* SCM Press 1993

Kuschel, Karl-Josef, *Laughter. A Theological Reflection,* SCM Press 1994

Lessing, Doris, *Collected African Stories:* Vol. 1, *This Was the Old Chief's Country;* Vol. 2, *The Sun Between Their Feet,* Triad Panther Books, Granada Publishing, also Michael Joseph and Jonathan Cape 1973

Levi, Primo, *If This Is A Man,* Bodley Head 1966

Lischer, Richard, 'Preaching as the Church's Language', in Gail R. O'day and G. Thomas Long (eds.), *Listening to the Word. Studies in Honour of Fred B. Craddock,* Abingdon 1993, pp. 113–30

——, *A Theology of Preaching: The Dynamics of the Gospel* (1982), revised edition, Labyrinth Press 1992

Macleod, Ian, *Preaching on the Lord's Supper. Encounter with Christ*, Mowbrays 1990

Mandela, Nelson, *Long Walk to Freedom*, Little, Brown and Company 1994

Manson, T. W., *The Sayings of Jesus*, SCM Press 1949

Marriage, Alwyn, 'God of the Holy Humour', *Christian* 20, July/August 1990, pp. 5–7

McCreary, Alf, *Corrymeela – The Search for Peace*, Christian Journals 1975

McKim, Donald M., *The Bible in Theology and Preaching. How Preachers Use Scripture*, Abingdon Press (1985) [2]1993

Morton, Margaret, *The Tunnel*, Yale University Press 1996

Mosala, Itumeleng J., *Biblical Hermeneutics and Black Theology in South Africa*, Eerdmans 1989

——, *The Unquestionable Right to be Free*, Orbis Books 1986

Mowvley, Harry, *Guide to Old Testament Prophecy*, Lutterworth Press 1979

Murray, Robert S. J., *Exegesis and Imagination*, Ethel M. Wood Lecture, University of London 1988

O'Day, Gail R., and G. Thomas Long (eds.), *Listening to the Word. Studies in Honour of Fred B. Craddock*, Abingdon Press 1993

Osborne, John, *A Better Class of Person*, Faber and Faber and Penguin Books 1982

Pilger, John, *Heroes*, Jonathan Cape and Pan Books 1986

——, *A Secret Country*, Vintage 1989

——, *Distant Voices*, Vintage 1992

Powell, Mark Allen, *What is Narrative Criticism?* SPCK 1993

Promise of His Glory, The, Mowbray and Church House Publishing 1991

Radday, Yehuda T., and Athalya Brenner, *On Humour and Comic in the Hebrew Bible*, Sheffield Academic Press 1990

Rogerson, John, *Genesis 1–11*, Sheffield Academic Press 1991

Rose, Lois and Stephen, *The Shattered Ring*, SCM Press 1970

Rowland, Christopher and Mark Corner, *Liberating Exegesis: the Challenge of Liberation Theology to Biblical Studies*, SPCK 1990

Russell, Willy, *Blood Brothers*, London 1985

Saint-Exupéry, Antoine de, *The Little Prince*, Heinemann 1945 and Mammoth Paperback 1991

Smith, Christine, *Preaching as Weeping, Confession, and Resistance.*

Radical Responses to Evil, Westminster/John Knox Press 1992

Solzhenitsyn, Alexander, *Candle in the Wind*, Bodley Head and OUP 1973

Song, C. S., *The Tears of Lady Meng. A Parable of People's Political Theology*, WCC 1981

Steinbeck, John, *East of Eden*, Heinemann 1952 and Mandarin Paperbacks 1990

Stewart, Douglas, *The Ark of God*, Carey Kingsgate Press 1961

Sugirtharajah, R. S. (ed.), *Voices from the Margin. Interpreting the Bible in the Third World*, SPCK 1991

Taylor, John V., *The Go-Between God*, SCM Press 1972

Tolstoy, Leo, *Resurrection*, Penguin Books 1966

——, *The Power of Darkness*, Constable 1914

Toth, Jennifer, *The Mole People*, Chicago Review Press 1995

Trible, Phyllis, *God and the Rhetoric of Sexuality*, SCM Press 1992

——, *Texts of Terror. Literary-Feminist Readings of Biblical Narratives*, SCM Press 1992

Turner, Steve, *Nice and Nasty*, Marshall, Morgan and Scott 1980

Walpole, Hugh, *The Herries Chronicle*, Macmillan 1939

Watson, Francis, *Text, Church and World: Biblical Interpretation in Theological Perspective*, T. & T. Clark 1994

—— (ed.), *The Open Text. New Directions for Biblical Studies?*, SCM Press 1993

Wilde, Oscar, 'The Ballad of Reading Gaol', in *Complete Works of Oscar Wilde*, HarperCollins 1994, pp. 883–99

Williams, H. A., *Tensions*, Collins 1976

Wilson, Paul Scott, 'Beyond Narrative: Imagination in the Sermon', in Gail R. O'Day and Thomas G. Long (eds.), *Listening to the Word. Studies in Honour of Fred B. Craddock*, Abingdon Press 1993, pp. 113–30

Zimmermann, Wolf-Dieter and Ronald Gregor Smith, *I Knew Dietrich Bonhoeffer*, Collins 1966.

Articles

Bostock, Gerald, 'Questions People Ask 6. Many Churches – One God?', in *Expository Times*, 107/4, January 1996, pp. 100–4

Clines, David J. A., 'The Ten Commandments, Reading from Left to Right', subsequently published in id., *Interested Parties: The Ideology of Writers and Readers of the Hebrew Bible*, JSOT Supplement Series 205, Sheffield 1995

Goldfarb, Michael, 'Laughter and the Art of Survival', *The Guardian*, 26 July 1990, p. 21

Mesters, Carlos, 'Como se faz Theologia hoje no Brasil?' *Estudos Biblicos* 1, 1985, pp. 1ff.

——, 'The Use of the Bible in Christian Communities of the Common People', in Norman K. Gottwald (ed.), *The Bible and Liberation. Political and Social Hermeneutics*, pp. 119–33

Mosala, Itumeleng J., 'The Use of the Bible in Black Theology', and 'Biblical Hermeneutics of Liberation: the Case of Micah', in R. S. Sugirtharajah (ed.), *Voices from the Margin. Interpreting the Bible in the Third World*, pp. 50–60 and 104–116, previously published as one essay in a volume co-edited by Mosala, *The Unquestionable Right to be Free*, Orbis Books 1986

Notes

Preface

1. Subsequently published as *Tomorrow's Pulpit*.
2. Douglas Stewart, *The Ark of God*, was one of the first, but also Kay Baxter, *Speak What We Feel*; David Anderson, *The Tragic Protest*; and Lois and Stephen Rose, *The Shattered Ring*. John Taylor, *The Go-Between God*, and J. G. Davies, *Every Day God*, also developed some of the same ideas and took me beyond the theatre to other forms of literature and life.
3. This was not a performing group. It was a group of people who enjoyed watching good drama and who then met within ten to fourteen days to talk about what they had seen and to share their experiences and responses. A key person was Martin Preston, a Baptist minister living in Brighton and teaching English Literature at Dulwich College, and it was his interventions and interaction with other members of the group that I found invaluable.

Introduction: Making Something Happen

1. I am indebted to Robert Murray SJ, *Exegesis and Imagination*, p. 8, for this allusion.
2. This was the main argument of *Tomorrow's Pulpit*.
3. Franck, *The Zen of Seeing. Seeing/Drawing as Meditation*, pp. xivff.
4. Ibid., pp. 3ff.
5. Wordsworth, 'Ode on Intimations of Immortality'.

1. Beginning with the Bible

1. I take the period of prophetic activity as being roughly from the time of David to the early Christian era, including of course John the Baptist and Jesus himself, though recognizing that the 'golden' or formative period is probably no more than 250 years. Harry Mowvley (*Guide to Old Testament Prophecy*, pp. 37ff.) dates this period from 750 to 500 BC.
2. Paul Scott Wilson, below, pp. 132–3.

3. See below, pp. 133ff.

4. The Hebrew *dabhar* means 'deed' as well as 'word'; the Hebrews were much less aware of the distinction between the two than we are.

5. Mowvley, *Guide to Old Testament Prophecy*, p. 3, in making this distinction, goes on to point out that the prophets were nevertheless very much concerned with contemporary affairs and often were not slow to say what they thought was going to happen as a result, but usually in relation to events close at hand. The Greek *prophētēs* (which was used to translate the Hebrew *nabhi* in the LXX) meant literally 'one who speaks for another, especially for a deity' (Bernhard W. Anderson, *The Living World of the Old Testament*, p. 248). Hence the idea of the prophet as a spokesperson, a public speaker, an interpreter of the will of God.

6. II Sam. 11–12 and I Kings 21.

7. See below pp. 28–32.

8. The depth and the finer points of the story come out much more forcefully in Archie C. C. Lee, 'The David–Bathsheba Story and the Parable of Nathan', in R. S. Sugirtharajah (ed.), *Voices from the Margin. Interpreting the Bible in the Third World*, pp. 189–204, where he describes it as a parable that 'presents the people's case . . . a story told from the side of the poor', includes a section headed 'Monarchy of Service or Government of Exploitation', and pinpoints the way 'David listens to the case as though he is the judge attending a court hearing'.

9. Of course this story made its greatest impact at the point when it was in the press (*The Observer*, June 1994), but it is only meant to be illustrative. Stories like it are appearing all the time.

10. Each preacher and worshipper must learn to find his or her own. There is no shortage, but anyone who wants to read a book which might do for our day what some of the prophets did for theirs could do worse than turn to John Pilger, who is continually uncovering issues that the press, media and politicians would prefer us not to look at, and only too often drawing our attention to things many of us would prefer not to have to think about. See *Heroes*, *A Secret Country*, and *Distant Voices*.

11. Melanie Phillips, *The Guardian*, June 1994.

12. One's skill in both recognizing the contemporary prophet and finding suitable biblical parallels may be tested in this exercise, but it becomes easier to get on the wavelength once you cultivate the habit of reading the Bible regularly alongside the events of the day.

13. This is in fact ideal resource material for those preachers today who want 'to reflect on the wider social context in which we live our lives of faith' (see Christine Smith, *Preaching as Weeping, Confession, and Resistance. Radical Responses to Evil*, p. 1).

14. See Paul Scott Wilson, 'Beyond Narrative: Imagination in the Sermon', in Gail R. O'Day and G. Thomas Long (eds.), *Listening to the Word. Studies in Honour of Fred B. Craddock*, pp. 140f.

15. Three readings which focus themes may be Hos. 4.1–3 (judgment); 6.1–6 (repentance); and 11.1–4, 8–9 (forgiveness). For background see Graham I. Davies, *Hosea*.

16. A variation on this idea which may lead to developments in other directions is provided by the bishop's wife in Susan Howatch's *Absolute Truths* (p. 205). After describing in her diary the changes that have taken place in members of her prayer group, she reflects on changes in herself with the words, 'If I'm a number in a sum, any change in me will affect the other numbers in that we'll all add up to a different answer.'

17. For the basic idea and some of the background see Juan I. Alfaro, *Micah: Justice and Loyalty*, and Itumeleng J. Mosala, 'The Use of the Bible in Black Theology', and 'Biblical Hermeneutics of Liberation: the Case of Micah', in R. S. Sugirtharajah (ed.), *Voices from the Margin*, pp. 50–60 and 104–16, previously published as one essay in a volume co-edited by Mosala, *The Unquestionable Right to be Free*. See also Itumeleng J. Mosala, *Biblical Hermeneutics and Black Theology in South Africa*. Mosala's work also provides a good illustration of what happens when you come at a book like Micah from the standpoint of someone in South Africa rather than in the traditional Western setting.

18. By 'simple' people I do not mean the illiterate or uneducated, and certainly not the stupid, but people with no pretensions to theological learning or understanding and with an uncomplicated and ready appreciation of people and their lives, their conflicts, tensions, disappointments and hopes.

19. Charles R. Avila, *Peasant Theology. Reflections by the Filipino Peasants on their Process of Social Revolution*, Chapter 5 ('Of Birds and Fishes'), pp. 12ff.

20. The idea and inspiration, though not the detailed interpretation, came as a result of reading the poem 'Institutions', by Frances Young.

21. I Kings 18.20–46.

22. Hastings, *Dictionary of the Bible*, p. 500.

23. The fact that this sequence of events differs from the way in which the details are related in Kings may be attributed to poetic licence. We are after the mood and the feelings, not the historical detail.
24. Gen. 25.23.
25. In her regular column in *The Observer*, c. 1975.
26. Avila, *Peasant Theology*, pp. 3–11.
27. Cf the fourth planet belonging to a businessman who was busy counting the stars, which he claimed to 'own' because nobody else had claimed them, and he was the first person to think of it (Antoine de Saint-Exupéry, *The Little Prince*, pp. 41–5).
28. Isaiah 11.6.
29. Leo Tolstoy, *The Power of Darkness*, Vol. 2, p. 91.
30. John V. Taylor, *The Go-Between God*, p. 125.
31. Susan Howatch, *Absolute Truths*, pp. 366ff.
32. The older brother rather than the prodigal son (Luke 15) is an obvious example which many preachers have used.
33. The story might be even more enriched if it were read alongside the various emotional attachments between two fathers and their two sons (each) in Steinbeck's *East of Eden*, or related to the bishop's two sons in Susan Howatch, *Absolute Truths*.

2. Beginning with Life

1. Alf McCreary, *Corrymeela – The Search for Peace*, p. 62.
2. 'The Lord is in his holy temple; let all the earth keep silence before him!'
3. An alternative way of expressing this would have been through some lines found at the foot of a life-size statue of an African beast in the hall of the international airport in Lusaka, Zambia.

> Creatures of the wild
> we patronize them for their incompleteness,
> for their tragic fate of having taken form
> so far below ourselves,
> and therein we err, and greatly err.
> For the animal world shall not be measured by man.
> In a world older and more complete than ours
> they moved finished and complete,
> gifted with extensions of the senses
> we have lost or never attained,
> living by voices we shall never hear.
> They are not brethren,

they are not underlings,
they are other nations,
caught with ourselves in the net of life and time,
fellow prisoners of the splendour and travail of the earth

(Henry Beeston).

4. 'Blood, Sweat and Tears', in Steve Turner, *Nice and Nasty*, p. 17.
5. Quoted in Susan Howatch, *Absolute Truths*, p. 617, where the surrounding material may supply other ideas.
6. In most years similar comparisons could be made.
7. T. W. Manson, *The Sayings of Jesus*, p. 248.
8. Ibid.
9. Dan Hook, *Effective Preaching*, pp. 49–51.
10. Since it didn't, I could only work from Hook's story, with which I hope I have not taken too many liberties.
11. John 21.15–18.
12. Readers who wish to reflect further on this idea may be helped by reading Oscar Wilde, 'The Ballad of Reading Gaol'.

3. Beginning with Literature

1. Franz Kafka, 'The Metamorphosis', in *Stories 1904–1924*, pp. 89–146.
2. Ps. 22.6.
3. Luke 10.25–37.
4. C. S. Song, *The Tears of Lady Meng. A Parable of People's Political Theology*, pp. 1–23.
5. Ex. 1.8–14.
6. Ex. 1.15–21; 5.1–22.
7. Ex. 12.29–32.
8. I subsequently sent a copy of the sermon to the cast and asked for their comments on my interpretation. They in turn sought permission to publish it in their summer brochure and introduced it with the words, '. . . Beckett's thoughtful and provocative play . . . gave rise to a great deal of comment and discussion. One of the most surprising reactions came in the form of a sermon . . . We were so impressed that we asked the minister for permission to reproduce it. Further comment would be superfluous. Here it is.'
9. Mark 1.17.
10. John 12.25.
11. Made popular by Elton John in the mid-1970s and recently enjoying something of a revival.

12. Solzhenitsyn, *Candle in the Wind*.
13. Acts 16.16ff.
14. Norman Mailer's biography of Marilyn Monroe appeared about the same time as the song, and there was a fair amount of television coverage.
15. I Sam. 16.
16. His rich relative, Uncle Maurice, thinks he's mad and asks how he could possibly live in the desert 'with no gas, no electricity, no running water and no sewage system', and Alex replies, 'In candlelight, Uncle, your heart opens up. And when you go outside you have the wind blowing from the steppes and the smell of wild herbs! Ooh-ooh-ooh! And if there's no electricity, when the moon rises over the desert the whole universe is flooded with moonlight! – Don't you remember that, at least from when you were a child, Uncle? Why are you blinking like that, all popeyed?' (p. 26).
17. Possibly it is Alex who has the greater problem, and you wonder how much his heart is really in it: '. . . everything's ready for doing what you need,' he says, 'for making a fragile person into an unbending one. You hear me? Giving to a person a stable, serene character and mental imperturbability. You're not ill and you don't need treatment in the normal sense, but you are too sensitive and vulnerable. You need to be helped to live . . . Alda, dear, let's try it. Give me your hand to show you agree. It's for your sake! So that a tranquil smile shall never leave your face. You've had enough suffering, haven't you?' (p. 62).
18. Solzhenitsyn, *Candle in the Wind*, p. 85.
19. Ibid., p. 113.
20. Luke 11.35.

4. *Going on From Here*

1. *The Guardian*, 17 October 1995.
2. Carlos Mesters, 'Como se faz Theologia hoje no Brasil?', *Estudos Biblicos* 1, 1985, p. 10, quoted in Christopher Rowland and Mark Corner, *Liberating Exegesis: The Challenge of Liberation Theology to Biblical Studies*, pp. 35–41.
3. Carlos Mesters, 'The Use of the Bible in Christian Communities of the Common People', in Norman K. Gottwald (ed.), *The Bible and Liberation. Political and Social Hermeneutics*, pp. 119ff, especially pp. 128–9.
4. See above, pp. 18ff.

5. *The Promise of His Glory*, Year 2, Lectionary 1, Table 1 (p. 385).

6. 'These were the words of the Lord to me: Prophesy, man, against the shepherds of Israel; prophesy and say to them, "You shepherds, these are the words of the Lord God: How I hate the shepherds of Israel who care only for themselves! Should not the shepherd care for the sheep?"' (Ezek. 34.1–2).

7. Extracts from John Barrington, *Red Sky at Night*, pp. 97, 101, 106, 108 and 112 present a good picture of 'A Shepherd in Spring'.

8. 'Thus says the Lord of hosts, the God of Israel: Houses and fields and vineyards shall again be brought into this land.'

9. When I tackled this theme in the summer of 1994 it so happened that it was in the week when Mark Tully left the BBC. The media attention told its own story. After thirty years as a distinguished reporter, especially in India, his departure received more coverage there than it did here, and the manner of his going possibly spoke louder than anything he ever actually said. First he had earlier referred publicly to John Birt's BBC as 'an Orwellian empire run by fear'. Then he refused to sign a contract containing 'a gagging clause', preventing him from ever repeating that view or developing it. The man who had spent thirty years uncovering evil and corruption in India and other Asian countries was unable to hold his tongue when it came to evil and corruption in his own domain if he were to retain any personal integrity. But then Tully's whole training was to speak only in the old language of loyalty, duties, principles and moral purpose. Like many others, he found it impossible to live in a world where the new 'market-language' way of reporting was bound to the fear of losing your job. He said it was a whole way of making people frightened. People who hold power use it to intimidate others – often ruthlessly and with less and less regard for the limits laid down by custom and practice. Tully found himself fighting the down-sizers on behalf of the down-sized, the strippers on behalf of the stripped, and believed that to become part of it was to join in your own intimidation and in the intimidation of others. He saw the moral dimension of his work endangered by managers who did not even grasp that their staff may have other purposes beyond preserving their jobs and their salaries.

10. Nelson Mandela, *Long Walk to Freedom*, pp. 14–20.

11. Ibid., pp. 38–40.

12. Ibid., p. 39.

13. See above, pp. 58ff.

14. See below, pp. 114ff.

15. 'The Garden of God,' pp. 11–14.
16. 'God Expulsion', pp. 25–28.
17. 'The Risk', pp. 41–3.
18. 'The Grass-eater', pp. 69–73, using material from Robert Vavra and Fleur Cowles, *Tiger Flower*, Collins 1968.
19. 'The Scapegoat', pp. 62–5.
20. 'God's Tears', pp. 56–7.
21. Ex. 33.18–23.
22. Dennis, *Speaking of God*, pp. 15–17.
23. One way of cultivating the habit of story-telling is by reading short stories for pleasure and not necessarily stories as overtly biblical or theological as those of Dennis. There are many short stories which spark off the imagination, and again, linked with other suitable material, provide the basis for preaching. The choice is obviously personal, but Doris Lessing's *Collected African Stories* provide a good example of the genre and have the added merit that they enable us to see ourselves and the world through the eyes of another culture. The reader might begin with 'Little Tembi' (Vol. 1) and 'The Sun Between their Feet (Vol. 2). Short stories of a different kind but again reflecting a different culture are Franz Kafka, *Stories 1904–1924*, or (for those looking for something longer) Franz Kafka, *The Complete Novels*.
24. 'The Garden of God', pp. 11–14.
25. Gen. 21.6.
26. Harry Williams, *Tensions*, pp. 116ff.
27. Alwyn Marriage, 'God of the Holy Humour', in *Christian*, 20, July/August 1990, pp. 5–7. The whole of this issue was devoted to humour. Cf. also Karl-Josef Kuschel, *Laughter. A Theological Reflection*.
28. See Michael Goldfarb, 'Laughter and the Art of Survival', in *The Guardian*, 26 July 1990, p. 21, and Radday and Brenner, *On Humour and Comic in the Hebrew Bible*.
29. Cf. Harvey Cox, *The Feast of Fools*.
30. By Hugh Walpole.
31. Trevor Dennis, *Lo and Behold! The Power of Old Testament Storytelling*. See also his devotional studies on the Song of Songs in *Guidelines*, 23 May to 5 June 1994, Bible Reading Fellowship, Oxford.
32. Dennis, *Lo and Behold!*, p. 3.
33. Ibid., pp. 61ff.
34. Ibid., pp. 42ff.

35. Cf. my reference to Jeremiah (above p. 95).
36. Dennis, *Lo and Behold!*, p. 54.
37. Ibid., p. 45.
38. See David M. Gunn and Danna N. Fewell, *Narrative in the Hebrew Bible*, pp. 12–33, and John Rogerson, *Genesis 1–11*, pp. 33–5.
39. Steinbeck, *East of Eden*.
40. Larry J. Kreitzer, *The Old Testament in Fiction and Film*, pp. 94ff.
41. John 5.2–9.
42. Amos 8.1–2. The connection is a pun, the Hebrew word *qayits* (a basket of summer fruit) sounding similar to *qets* (the end).
43. See above, pp. 53f.
44. 'The Naming of Cats' (*Old Possum's Book of Practical Cats*), in T. S. Eliot, *Complete Poems and Plays*, p. 209, especially the lines
    'You may think at first I'm as mad as a hatter
    When I tell you, a cat must have THREE DIFFERENT NAMES.'
45. Ex. 3.13–15 (NRSV). Parallel New Testament readings might be Phil. 2.1–11 and Matt. 16.13–20.
46. Cf. Gerald Bostock, 'Questions People Ask 6. Many Churches – One God?', in *Expository Times* 107/4, January 1996, pp. 100–4.
47. Eph. 6.12.
48. See Barbara Greene and Victor Gollancz, *God of a Hundred Names: Prayers of Many Peoples and Creeds*. Notice especially the Old Egyptian Prayer on p. 5 and the philosophy behind the book (p. 9): 'From amidst diversified and often warring creeds: over a vast span of history: in the language of many a tribe and many a nation: out of the mouths of the learned and simple, the lowly and great: despite oceans of bloodshed, and torturing humanities, and persecutions unspeakable – the single voice of a greater Humanity rises confidently to heaven, saying, "We adore thee, who art One and who art Love: and it is in unity and love that we would live together, doing Thy will".'
49. In *The Complete Novels*.
50. Read Hans Küng, *Credo*, pp. 89ff.
51. 'The Cross: Horizontal and Vertical', in Joseph G. Donders, *Jesus the Stranger*, pp. 172–6. Cf. Dennis's idea of Eden as the place where you were always liable to bump into God in the cool of the day, a privilege lost at the Fall but always holding out the possibility of re-instatement (*Lo and Behold!*, p. 21).
52. See above, pp. 22–3.
53. 'By gracious powers, so wonderfully sheltered', written for New

Year 1945, so shortly before his execution, translated by F. Pratt Green and Keith Clements, in *Baptist Praise and Worship*, p. 117.

54. Eberhard Bethge, Renate Bethge and Christian Gemmels (eds.), *Dietrich Bonhoeffer, A Life in Pictures*, is a good example. But see also Wolf-Dieter Zimmermann and Ronald Gregor Smith, *I Knew Dietrich Bonhoeffer*; Eberhard Bethge, *Dietrich Bonhoeffer. Theologian, Christian, Contemporary*; Otto Dudzus, *Bonhoeffer for a New Generation*.

55. Carlos Christo, *Letters from a Prisoner of Conscience*, pp. 125-7. For additional or alternative material use some of the experiences of people living in the New York Subway and reported in Jennifer Toth, *The Mole People*, and Margaret Morton, *The Tunnel*.

56. See above, pp. 58ff., 99.

57. The use of the word 'parable' must not mislead us at this point. There is no suggestion that what follows should be regarded as a satisfactory way of handling the parables of Jesus.

58. If we look at the story from Katusha's point of view we see how before Nekhlyudov's arrival, even as a servant, she was free, whereas after that third kiss she was a slave, and when he visits her in prison after the sentence she can no longer see the kind, loving youth she once knew. All she can see is the cruel exploiter and how by turning her into a prostitute he has changed her attitude to men in a way that is irreversible (*Resurrection*, pp. 197, 202).

59. When the Truth Commission was set up in South Africa under the chairmanship of Archbishop Tutu in 1995, following the end of apartheid, there were those who argued against it on the grounds that it was liable to drag up many things that would be better forgotten. Tuto's response was that South Africa needed the Truth Commission because it was important that they 'look the beast in the eye', so that afterwards they could move forward together (Phillip van Niekerk, writing in *The Observer*, 24 December 1995).

60. You are therefore no longer a slave but a son, and if a son, then also by God's own act an heir (Gal. 4.7).

61. Luke 7.36-48, Ex. 18.1-9, Mark 14.43-46.

62. *The Observer*, 18 February 1996.

63. Gen. 18.12; 21.6.

64. Dan. 3.

65. Jer. 32.7-8, 25.

66. The musical opens with the lines: 'Here in Anatevka you may say that every one of us is a fiddler on the roof, trying to scratch out a pleasant, simple tune without breaking his neck. It isn't easy. You

may ask, why do we stay up here if it is so dangerous? Well, we stay up here because Anatevka is our home. And how do we keep our balance? That I can answer in one word, Tradition.'

67. Rom. 8.37.
68. Mark 6.30–44.
69. Osborne, *A Better Class of Person*, pp. 65, 78.

5. *Changing Gear*

1. See above, p. 12.
2. Similar features appear in many sermons in the *Expository Times*, where a number of those in the Mowbrays series have also been published.
3. *Preaching at the Parish Communion* (all relating to the ASB Epistles and Gospels), *Preaching through the Christian Year, Preaching on Great Themes, Preaching on Favourite Hymns, Preaching through the Prophets* (...the Psalms ...the Life of Christ ... the Acts of the Apostles ...St Paul), *Preaching on the Holy Spirit, Preaching on the Lord's Supper*, and so on. Each volume contains about twenty-four sermons, mostly from one source, with no less than seven volumes from D. W. Cleverley Ford, who is also Series Editor. The length varies from 1,500 to 2,000 words (or fifteen to twenty minutes) and there is usually a text to begin with.
4. In the Introduction to *Preaching on Great Themes. Creation, Incarnation, Redemption and Resurrection.*
5. 'Preaching as the Church's Language', in Gail R. O'Day and G. Thomas Long (eds.), *Listening to the Word*, pp. 124–5.
6. Cleverley Ford, *Preaching on Great Themes*, pp. 1–5.
7. Ibid., pp. 9–13.
8. He does not say why, or for whom, it was difficult but it is perhaps worth noting that as a final sentence this is more than enough to kill any real impact the sermon might have made up to that point!
9. Ibid., pp. 35–40.
10. Lischer, *A Theology of Preaching: The Dynamics of the Gospel*, Preface. Cf. id., 'Preaching as the Church's Language', in Gail R. O'Day and G. Thomas Long (eds.), *Listening to the Word*, pp. 124–5.
11. Ibid.
12. Ibid., p. 37.
13. Id., 'Preaching as the Church's Language', p. 121.

14. See 'The Bag Lady' above, p. 58.
15. Dan Hook, 'Clarifying the Task', in *Effective Preaching*, p. 29.
16. Ibid., pp. 31f.
17. Ibid., pp. 46ff.
18. See above, pp. 125–9.
19. The reader may now like to compare the bag lady's concept of 'taking bread' (Hook, *Effective Preaching*, pp. 49–51, see above, pp. 58ff.), with any of the sermons on the same subject in Ian Macleod, *Preaching on the Lord's Supper. Encounter with Christ*, and perhaps to do better in the light of John Osborne's experience (see above, pp.120–2).
20. Smith, *Preaching as Weeping, Confession, and Resistance*, p. 1.
21. Paul Scott Wilson, 'Beyond Narrative: Imagination in the Sermon', in Gail R. O'Day and G. Thomas Long (eds.), *Listening to the Word*, pp. 131ff.
22. Ibid., pp. 140f.
23. The example Wilson gives is the text, 'Jesus used the absence of wine as an occasion to manifest God's glory'. If you then put this in the present ('Jesus comes to us in our need to manifest God's glory') you have an idea that may be a truth for our time.
24. Brueggemann, *The Bible and Postmodern Imagination*, pp. 62f.
25. The papers given at the conference were published in a book edited by Francis Watson, *The Open Text*.
26. *Text, Church and World: Biblical Interpretation in Theological Perspective*. 'The position developed in this book is, in one sense,' writes Watson (p. vii), 'a familiar one: that biblical interpretation should concern itself primarily with the theological issues raised by the biblical texts within our contemporary ecclesial, cultural and socio-political contexts. At a time when many former hermeneutical certainties are encountering sustained and effective challenge, the familiar but still controversial claim that biblical interpretation should no longer neglect its theological responsibilities is due for reformulation and restatement.'
27. Donald M. McKim, *The Bible in Theology and Preaching. How Preachers Use Scripture*.
28. The earlier book, for instance, had two sections on the different uses of scripture by the Roman Catholic and Protestant traditions, followed by chapters on liberal, fundamentalist, scholastic, neo-orthodox, neo-evangelical, existential, process, narrative and liberation theologies. The revised edition felt it necessary to add chapters on black, Asian and feminist theologies.

29. A good example is the way in which the Song of Songs has been interpreted and re-interpreted over the years: allegorical and symbolical interpretations going back to antiquity, dramatic inter- pretations dating from the fourth century, weddings and wedding week theories from Wetzstein at the end of the nineteenth century, structural interpretations mainly through the application of form criticism within the last few decades, literal interpretations in an attempt to find a literary cohesion for the book and, most recently, feminist interpretations (see A. Brenner, *The Song of Songs*, pp. 67–77, 87–93). For a similar example of the way in which Genesis 4 has been interpreted over 2,000 years see David M. Gunn and Danna Nolan Fewell, *Narrative in the Hebrew Bible*, pp. 12–33.

30. Watson, *Text, Church and World*, passim.

31. 'The Ten Commandments, Reading from Left to Right', subsequ- ently published in David J. A. Clines, *Interested Parties: The Ideology of Writers and Readers of the Hebrew Bible*, JSOT Supplement Series 205, pp. 26–45. 'Reading from right to left' denotes falling in with the Hebrew way of reading and adopting the world view of the author. 'Reading from left to right' means standing outside that world and raising questions of value and validity (p. 26).

32. Clines profiles the people with these values more fully, but they are those who have an interest in maintaining and defending what the Ten Commandments are there to maintain and defend. They are the haves who want to pretend that everyone in society is equal. 'It makes them more comfortable not to have to worry that their privilege may be the cause of other people's poverty; and, if the underprivileged can be made to believe in this equality, it lessens the chances of social friction. The poor, however, are not under the illusion that they are the brothers of neighbours or equals of the rich' (pp. 32ff).

33. R. S. Sugirtharajah (ed.), *Voices from the Margin*, p. 1.

34. Ibid., p. 2.

35. Ibid., p. 3.

36. Entries to this volume had to pass three tests. One, the writers had to identify with contextual concerns and take them seriously in their biblical reflections. Two, they had to transcend the traditional historical-critical tools or employ indigenous tools to release the text. Three, the 'people's commentaries' had to speak from the realities of the vulnerable and the under-privileged. The result is a

volume with five kinds of material, each of which reflects something different as well as something new (pp. 4–6):

1. Essays which challenge Euro-American exegesis and offer something more appropriate to their own social and cultural circumstances.

2. Samples of work from Third World writers using some traditional tools and some indigenous tools to look at the text afresh.

3. Essays showing how one narrative can lend itself to several readings.

4. Essays dealing with issues that are pertinent to Asians and Africans who are living as minorities among people who possess their own sacred books.

5. Unique contributions from ordinary people in Asia, Africa and Latin America. These are from people with one foot in the academy and the other in the community or from people at the grassroots who want to recover the biblical texts from other-worldly, ahistorical and apolitical readings for the empowerment of the community.

37. For example, see how when Micah is read through the eyes of a South African who sees it as a product of the class struggle it is distinctly different from the three-fold Western interpretation of the book based on Micah 6.8, or what happens to the social history of the Hebrews when put alongside that of the Korean *minjung* by a Korean biblical scholar.

38. A special issue of the journal on 'Class Origins and Class Readings of the Bible' (Vol. II, nos. 2–3) published by Radical Religion.

39. *The Bible and Liberation: Political and Social Hermeneutics.*

40. Norman K. Gottwald (ed.), *The Bible and Liberation: Political and Social Hermeneutics*, p. 1.

41. Rowland and Corner, *Liberating Exegesis: The Challenge of Liberation Theology to Biblical Studies.* For a more systematic approach to sociological and political issues as they arise in the Old Testament see Anthony R. Ceresko, *Introduction to the Old Testament. A Liberation Perspective.*

42. Ibid., p. 2.

43. Ibid., pp. 38ff. Whilst acknowledging liberation theology's debt to the Enlightenment and the fact that in its early days the historical-critical method led to a revival of interest in the Bible, Mesters nevertheless feels that in recent years much technical scholarship has had the effect of only distancing the Bible from the lives of

ordinary people. This has therefore given rise at the grass-roots to a new method of reading the Bible with a threefold emphasis: one, to see and begin with one's own experience, which for most people in Latin America means poverty; two, to judge or understand the reason for the experience and compare it with the story of deliverance from oppression in the Bible; three, to act. The Bible for Mesters is not just about past history. It is more a mirror to be held up to reflect the story of today and give it new perspective. With this tool the poor people of Latin America have therefore taken the Bible into their own hands and not only to read it but to act on it. The story of the Exodus is *their* story. Something has happened here too. See also Mesters, 'The Use of the Bible in Christian Communities of the Common People', in Gottwald (ed.), *The Bible and Liberation*, pp. 119–33.

44. The sub-title is 'Literary-Feminist Readings of Biblical Narratives'.

45. Hagar, Tamar, an Unnamed Woman (Judg. 19) and the daughter of Jephthah. In Gen. 16, for example, power belongs to Sarai, the subject of action, whereas powerlessness marks Hagar the object, and Abram, far from being the mighty patriarch to whom we are accustomed, becomes 'the silent, acquiescent and minor figure in a drama between two women' (pp. 10–11). The question she raises is how this ever managed to be seen as the story of Abram, when it is so much the story of Sarai and Hagar, and how Hagar could be so overlooked when she is the first person to receive an annunciation, an Egyptian who is the prototype of special mothers in Israel (pp. 14–16).

46. The same might be said of her interpretation of Gen. 2–3 as summarized by John Rogerson, *Genesis 1–11*, pp. 35–8, where other feminist interpretations of the same incident are also to be found.

47. For a summary of this approach see Robert Alter and Frank Kermode (eds.), *The Literary Guide to the Bible*, pp. 1–8. The literature is already vast and growing rapidly, but readers wishing to get a 'feel' for the idea may refer to Robert Alter, *The World of Biblical Literature*; David M. Gunn and Danna Nolan Fewell, *Narrative in the Hebrew Bible*; Mark Allen Powell, *What is Narrative Criticism?*.

48. Powell, *Narrative Criticism*, p. ix.

49. Alter, *The World of Biblical Literature*, p. 46.

50. This point is recognized by Powell, *Narrative Criticism*, p. 103,

who then proceeds to give preachers a set of questions which they may ask of an 'episode' if they wish to handle it from the point of view of narrative criticism.

51. Alter, *The World of Biblical Literature*, pp. 107ff. For example, he suggests that to the Hebrew ear the use of the word *tevah* for the ark in which Moses was placed (Ex. 2.3) would immediately call to mind the Noah story and so indicate that what Moses was about was a new beginning. Similarly, the words of Amnon, 'Take everyone out from before me' (II Sam. 13.9), when he is preparing to rape his half-sister Tamar, would call to mind the identical words used by Joseph (Gen. 45.1) when he wants to tell his brothers who he is. One is a great moment of fraternal reconciliation, the other a prologue to sexual violation of the fraternal bond. Similarly, the four (Hebrew) words of lust, 'Come lie with me, my sister', would echo the two-word (in Hebrew) speech of Potiphar's wife to Joseph, 'Lie with me' (Gen. 39.7). Cf. Stephen Bigger, *Creating the Old Testament. The Emergence of the Hebrew Bible*, pp. 51–81.

Additional Notes on Sources and Settings

1. The word 'overall' is important. What it means is that over a given year a balanced number of biblical passages will have been covered. Theoretically, a balanced number of theological ideas will also have been addressed. But there is nothing to ensure that any particular sermon will be a balanced sermon or indeed that there is a balanced theological approach to whatever comes. Biblical literalists are still biblical literalists, evangelicals still evangelicals and so on, and they all have their own 'hobby horses', usually much more obviously recognizable to their congregation than to themselves, and the lectionary is no safeguard against it.

2. I acknowledge that these are generalizations, and that there are many exceptions, but since I am simply trying to appreciate the differences in general and not arguing the case, the picture may be considered acceptable.

Acknowledgment

I am grateful to A. P. Watt Ltd on behalf of Steve Turner to quote the poem 'Blood, Sweat and Tears' which appears on p.45.

Index

As far as possible entries are confined to those items which are not readily accessible through the Table of Contents or the Bibliography. References in the notes, therefore, are not normally included where there is already an entry in the main text.

People

Solzhenitsyn, Alexander, 87, 160, 162

Song, C. S., 160

Spurgeon, C. S., 123

Steinbeck, John, 102–3, 159

Stewart, Douglas, 156

Surgirtharajah, R. S., 157, 158, 168

Taylor, John V., 36–7, 156, 159

Tolstoy, Leo, 36–7, 116, 159

Toth, Jennifer, 165

Trible, Phyllis, 139

Tully, Mark, 162

Turner, Steve, 160

Tutu, Desmond, 26, 165

Walpole, Hugh, 101, 163

Watson, Francis, 134, 135, 167, 168

Webber, Andrew Lloyd, 104

Webster, Alan, 122

Weil, Simone, 107

Wesley, John, 123

Whitehorn, Katharine, 33

Williams, H. A., 101, 163

Wilson, Paul Scott, 132, 158, 167

Wordsworth, William, 7

Xhosa poet, 98–9

Yeltsin, Boris, 61

Young, Frances, 32, 158

Zimmerman, Wolf-Dieter, 165

Bible References

Genesis	2–3, 170	Judges	19, 170
	4, 102	I Samuel	16, 161
	16,170	II Samuel	11–12, 157
	18.12, 165		13.9, 171
	21.6, 163, 165	I Kings	18.20–46, 157
	25.23, 159		21, 157
	39.7, 171	Job	1–37, 107
	45.1, 171		23.1–12, 106
Exodus	1.8–14, 160	Psalms	23, 93
	1.15–21, 160		137, 96
	2.3, 171		149, 108
	3.13–15, 164	Isaiah	1–39, 17
	5.1–22, 160		6, 97
	3.15, 105		11.6, 159
	12.29–32, 160		24.5, 111
	16, 101		40.5, 111
	18.1–9, 165		53, 79
	33.18–23, 163	Jeremiah	32.7–8, 25, 165
Numbers	11, 101		32.15, 95–6

Subjects

Places

Bible Characters